VOODOO FIRE IN HAITI

Clara Ely

Eleanor Seymour

SHE STOOD FOR A MOMENT—A PERFECT STATUE IN BRONZE

RICHARD A. LOEDERER

VOODOO FIRE IN HAITI

TRANSLATED BY DESMOND IVO VESEY
WITH ILLUSTRATIONS BY THE AUTHOR

THE LITERARY GUILD, NEW YORK

PRINTED AT THE *Country Life Press*, GARDEN CITY, N. Y., U. S. A.

FIRST EDITION

ACKNOWLEDGMENTS

The author is indebted to John W. Vandercook for permission to adapt certain scenes from his book, *Black Majesty*, in the reconstruction of the life of King Christophe in Chapter IX of this book.

Other authorities consulted for historical and ethnological facts include:

Louis Gentil Tippenhauer—*Die Insel Haiti*, 1893
Sir Spencer St. John—*The Black Republic*, about 1880
Hasketh Prichard—*Where Black Rules White*, 1900
W. W. Harvey—*Sketches of Haiti*, 1827
Charles Mackenzie—*Notes on Haiti*, 1830
James Redpath—*A Guide to Haiti*, 1860
F. A. Ober—*A Guide to the West Indies*, 1914

Also, thanks are due a host of friends in Haiti who generously opened to the author doors to the vast storehouse of story and legend ordinarily hidden behind Haitian reticence.

Richard A. Loederer.

CONTENTS

CHAPTER PAGE

I CONGO BEAN STEW 1

II IN CARIBBEAN WATERS 24

III MASSACRE RIVER 43

IV JUNGLE MAGIC 64

V TROPICAL FEVER 86

VI MON REPOS 105

VII POLYCHROMATA

Port-au-Prince 123

Pétionville 141

Cap Haitien *143*
Petit Anse *147*
Grand Rivière *148*
Bahón *151*
Anse Rouge *156*
Plaine de Gonaïves *163*
St. Marc *166*
Miragoâne *167*
Aux Cayes *168*
Jérémie *171*
Coraïl *176*
Bizóton *179*
VIII LA FERRIÈRE *197*
IX KING CHRISTOPHE OF HAITI *228*
X BLACK MAGIC *248*
XI VOODOO FIRE *265*

ILLUSTRATIONS

She stood for a moment—a perfect statue in bronze *Frontispiece*

PAGE

Endless slave caravans wound their mournful way through the African bush *13*

The day was nearly over *39*

Then his galleon vanished round the bend *45*

Every day, at precisely the same hour, the heavens opened their sluices *55*

This reservoir of tropical nature seemed to be monstrous and inexhaustible *59*

Two toucans . . . settled on a branch and peered at me *69*

When opportunity offered I set up my easel *73*

The sea, an unruffled sheet of quicksilver, sent tired little ripples over the baking sand *137*

I saw the naked figure of a young negress *145*

Bamboo huts standing on stakes above the water *153*

In the doorway appeared a young negress *159*

Young negroes with their Port-au-Princesses glided over the floor *185*

A full-blooded negress appeared suddenly in the middle of the room *189*

Electrified into ecstatic motion *193*

An edifice of gigantic proportions, noble in its architectural conception *201*

Perched on the mountain peak—tremendous and appalling—the Citadel of King Christophe *215*

I wandered along the highest edge of the roof *225*

Fear must be planted in the people. Fear made them docile and through fear they could achieve the impossible *233*

In front of the hut was a pole with a bleached horse skull on the top *249*

The young negro when he woos a girl; a typical example of the innocent, naked eroticism of the African native *259*

VOODOO FIRE IN HAITI

THE MAMALOI

I. CONGO BEAN STEW

IN THE beginning it was like that—palm groves and thirsty white beaches and the shadowy dark mountains beyond. Lying in the clear pagan air, an unknown island untrodden by the foot of a white man, that was to be one of the great landmarks in the history of colonization.

Columbus was exploring westwards in search of a new continent. Months had passed and still there was no sight of land; the sailors were becoming mutinous, food was scarce, and then, one momentous day, came the welcome shout of "Land ahoy!" Their months of hardship were at an end.

And Columbus landed there; that much is known; but his records are not explicit as to whether he stayed much longer than to unfurl the Spanish flag and christen his new discovery

Hispaniola. The great explorer was still unsatisfied. He knew he had not yet reached his goal, and so, despite the wishes of his crew, who, it is certain, felt their long search to be over, he set sail and headed still further westwards.

How wonderful it must have been—the white beaches and the green palms and the blue-gray mountains beyond. Well —it is still like that today, but Haiti, as the island is now called, looks back on the past few centuries of her history with a bloodstained face. A whole dark chapter separates the old Hispaniola from the present day. Those were years filled with merciless fighting and cruel carnage; with the foul butchery of the entire white population by the frenzied negroes. In those days the clean white beaches ran red with blood. It was a holocaust of murder and primeval madness. A seeming record of unrelieved brutality; yet even a white man may come to understand, as I did later, the terrible wrongs that filled the blacks with such uncontrollable blood-lust, and caused them to set up an independent Black Republic.

The tales of tropical cruelties, tropical death, and tropical disease still act as a powerful deterrent to the casual traveler and Haiti has ever proved an inhospitable soil to the majority of its white visitors. It must be confessed therefore that it was not without some slight misgivings that I determined to visit and explore this strange country; to try and discover how much, if any, was true of the rumors of secret cults, black magic, and human sacrifices which were reported to exist in present-day Haiti.

It was on a bitterly cold, gloomy afternoon that the Dutch West Indian mail steamer, S.S. *Commewyne* throbbed uneasily through the fog that lay over New York Bay. As I peered through the murk, I distinguished for a moment the vast shadowy outline of the Statue of Liberty which loomed up and quickly vanished astern, merging into the universal canopy of darkness. Over the Narrows and on the sea beyond, night had already fallen.

The first thing I did after stowing my bags in my cabin was to go below and study the passenger list. From this I learned that I had seven fellow-travelers aboard. I waited patiently to see what they were like. Among the first to appear were two animal dealers, father and son, who were off to the wilds of the Orinoco to replenish the stock of their New York "house." The next arrivals were a friendly Dutch couple, obviously overjoyed to be traveling on a boat flying their national flag. In the course of conversation it transpired that they were bound for Paramaribo, where the husband owned an extensive plantation, the management of which, so he gave us to understand, was a full-time job; at any rate, it formed the whole sum and total of his conversation. That is, except on one occasion, when he remarked to me with tears in his eyes and apropos of nothing that his tropical home always greeted him when he was still some hundred miles from the coast. I naturally thought that he was indulging in a flight of phantasy, until he explained to me that the browny-red waters of the Surinam, the great river of Guiana, sweep miles out into the ocean before they lose their distinctive coloring. . . .

And then there was Sir Joshua Higginbotham. He was a "character," a lean, elderly Englishman of a type one often meets in the remotest corners of the earth: hard-bitten, leathery, full of little mannerisms, and yet charming in his eccentricity. He could talk for hours on almost any subject one cared to mention, and, such was his intimate and extensive knowledge, he was never boring. In the course of his life he had traveled widely, and he declared that he knew the West Indies as well as his own home.

The remaining two passengers were pure-blooded negroes who with their ultra-European bearing and appearance were both incongruous and entertaining. I was astonished at their elegance and education, but my amazement reached its climax when one day—arrayed in morning-coats of the very latest cut—they informed me that they had just graduated as doctors from the Pasteur Institute in Paris, and that they had devoted four years to a specialized study of dermatology. They were now returning to their native country, Haiti, in order to put their newly acquired knowledge into practice. They were extraordinarily friendly and gave me a unique opportunity of studying at close quarters two very fine representatives of the black aristocracy of the Republic.

Their western culture lay deeper than might at first sight have been expected and on only one occasion did the primitive African break through the shell of civilized convention. When someone put a record on the ship's gramophone the studied calm of the two black stoics vanished. Consciousness of rhythm submerged the veneer of civilization. Indeed, so strong was the primitive urge, that a complete physical change transformed their bodies. Flesh and bone became flexible; quivering ecstatically in response to the tinny tune. Through their long thin hands the music seemed to surge, compelling response in shoulders, hips and thighs—swaying, flexing, vibrating, in complete surrender to the throbbing rhythm. For the first time I realized what *rhythm* meant to the negro. It was a revelation.

I leant over the rail and watched the creaming breakers race away astern. Our little steamer was wallowing through the boiling seas, head down against the storm which was driving over us. Since morning the ocean had changed from lapping turquoise wavelets to angry black combers which took their colors from the threatening clouds above. An undeniable thrill of adventure ran through me as I thought of the strange land for which I was bound.

Then the first gong rang for dinner and I went to get ready.

During meals, at which we all forgathered, there was always a continuous flow of conversation, usually concerning the miraculous adventures which had befallen one or other of the party. It mattered not whether the tale had any foundation on fact: the narrator was always sure of an appreciative audience as long as the story came within the bounds of credibility. In this manner our little group of travelers, which certainly contained some very diverse elements, struck up that swift companionship that is only to be found in lonely parts of the world or on long sea voyages. Each individual was sufficient unto himself and had his own special privacy, and yet there existed an indefinable sense of community: maybe it was the sudden and complete change from every-day existence to this new life, or, more probably, the realization, perhaps for the first time, of an infinite loneliness only to be experienced beyond the far brink of civilization.

On this particular evening, and in spite of the heavy weather, all the passengers were present when the captain took his place. From the sideboard came the clatter of stacked crockery. The plates, glasses, and cutlery which lay before us were prevented from sliding into our laps by a wooden frame which the steward had fixed round the sides of the table. The soup, a watery and tinned variety, slopped over the plate with every roll of the ship; in fact, more landed on the tablecloth than ever reached my mouth. The fresh air and motion of the ship had made me hungry, and so unsatisfied by the two precarious spoonfuls of soup I had managed to swallow, I glanced at the menu to see what the pièce de resistance of the evening was to be. But before I had time to satisfy my greedy curiosity, the captain addressed me, and I continued to talk to him until the steward arrived with a large covered casserole from which he removed the lid, releasing a most appetizing odor. At the same moment he offered the dish to the man sitting on the right of Sir Joshua Higginbotham.

I picked up the menu again and this time managed to decipher the steward's spidery handwriting. *Congo Bean Stew.* A curious name. The concoction was one much favored by the Dutch, and consisted of lamb, cooked in a thick brown bean sauce, and garnished with potatoes and carrots. Sir Joshua, who was sitting opposite to me, gazed at this delicacy with unconcealed disgust. He waved the steward away and muttered: "Good God! I couldn't eat this; the very sight of it has spoilt my appetite." Then he turned to the captain and said, abruptly: "I hope you'll excuse me. It's unpleasantly hot down here," at which utterance he jumped up from the table and hurried out of the saloon. In spite of unconvincing efforts at control, our curiosity was plainly revealed as we shot inquiring glances at one another. The stolid Dutchman merely shrugged his shoulders and drained his glass of beer, while a broad grin spread over the captain's face as he remarked to the world at large: "Tchya—even an old globe-trotter is sometimes seasick."

I wondered at Higginbotham's behavior, for the bean stew was delicious and the juicy lumps of meat possessed an appetizingly spicy flavor, although the sauce was slightly on the sweet side. Still, young lamb should never be despised! By the time dessert arrived we had forgotten all about Sir Joshua and his strange behavior, and an animated conversation was again in full swing.

Outside, the weather was, if possible, becoming worse. As soon as we rounded Cape Hatteras, the northwester caught us on our beam and the *Commewyne* alternately pointed her bows at the bed of the ocean and lifted them towards the stars. Seen from the bridge there might be something magnificent in the way the giant waves reared and combed, and fell seething across the boat deck; but here below every bolt and bulkhead creaked and strained to the breaking point as the floundering vessel hung suspended before she climbed or sank. I had a thrilling view through the porthole, where scarcely two inches of glass separated us from the maelstrom of wind and sea. It was a very unstable world outside. There seemed to be no ordained place for the water; one minute the surface of the sea lay far below, and the next it had risen high above our heads. At odd moments the porthole was completely submerged, giving one the sensation of being in a submarine, especially when fishes swam against the glass. At last a sailor came in and closed all the portholes with heavy iron deadlights, clamping them fast with a key. He was shortly followed by an officer in streaming oilskins who called the captain out.

In a fit of hardihood I went to the purser and borrowed from him a full-length mackintosh and a sou'wester. After I had wrapped myself up, I tried to go outside but the door refused to open. It was held fast shut by the force of the gale. I tugged fiercely at the handle without avail. Then the ship veered suddenly and the door flew back with such unexpectedness that I measured my length on the deck. In complete darkness I struggled to my feet and guided by a guard rail, groped my way to the companion ladder which led to the bridge. Dark, closely muffled figures staggered up and down, scarcely visible in the inadequate glow of a hurricane lamp. Two of the mulatto crew stood in the wheelhouse, facing one another, silent, and, as far as possible, motionless. Their fingers glided over the spokes when the wheel spun, and the chain clattered metallically in its guide. In the charthouse an officer bent over his maps as he manipulated dividers and ruler.

Seen from above, the waves looked even more immense than before. They drove towards us house-high and the ship shook under the dull impact of their weight. The *Commewyne* was battling magnificently against what seemed to me to be invincible odds. Up and up rose the bows to their zenith in the black skies; a breathless pause as they hung ponderously in space, and then down, down into the very nadir of the seas. Each time I thought the ship must crumple up as another wave struck her sides, booming hollowly and throwing its creamy torrents over the deck. In a temporary lull the throb of the engines could be felt. Only once had the stern been so high that the engines raced before the water closed round the screws. I prayed that that would not occur again!

During an unusually long pause I began counting the seconds before the next crash, when suddenly, for no apparent reason, the sea got up on end and poured an avalanche of water over me and the ship. A boat was torn from its davits and swept overboard, and when the water had poured away I noticed that a ventilator was missing and two iron stanchions were bent like candles over a fire. Completely soaked and shivering like a drowned rat, I struggled back to my cabin, where I found my suitcases, trunks, paint-box, and toilet equipment piled in a rich confusion on the floor. They could stay there! Leaving everything as it lay I peeled off my wet clothes, wrapped myself in a blanket, and scrambled into my wildly heaving bunk.

. . . .

Eight bells rang out from the bridge.

"Eight bells," shouted the lookout in the crow's nest. A lovely Sunday morning greeted me as I stepped out on deck into the pleasant warmth of an early tropical sun. The fury of the previous night had completely blown itself out, and the still heaving seas shone ultramarine and gold, a perfect scene set by nature to prepare us for the exuberant beauty of the tropics. Drifting masses of brown sargasso weed showed plainly that we had reached the turning point of the great, warm stream where it sweeps out of the Gulf of Mexico. A school of dolphins plunged beside us, rolling gracefully over on the waves. Flying fish skimmed the waters in glittering flashes of silver. Having heard that these fish are said to use their fins like a bird uses its wings, I studied them through a pair of binoculars but failed to distinguish the slightest movement that might substantiate this theory.

In the distance emerald-green shallows were stretching out towards us. Beyond them lay silvery curves of sand and the faint blue hill of San Salvador. We were sailing in historic waters, for it was near here that Columbus caught his first glimpse of the New World. Intent on greater things, the old adventurer had changed his course, and sailed along the path which we were now following.

As I watched the receding shores, the lanky figure of Sir Joshua Higginbotham came and leant over the rail beside me. For a while he gazed steadfastly at the island, now a faint smudge above the waves; then he lowered his telescope and shut it with a snap. In answer to my inquiry as to how he was feeling, he turned sharply towards me:

"You thought I was feeling sick yesterday evening?"

The question was posed in such a downright manner that it obviously needed no answer, and receiving none from me he went on: "No, sir, I have *never* been seasick, and as far as I know I never shall be. It would require something infinitely more unpleasant than a slight sea to spoil *my* appetite. I fear the company may have thought me rude last night. Maybe. But my reason for leaving the table was a good one, and a strange one, and one that I could never have explained at dinner. For if I had told you then and there the reason for my aversion to that stew, I should most certainly have offended the two negroes."

I confessed I could not see what Congo Bean Stew had got to do with the two black gentlemen from Haiti, whereupon he slid his telescope into its leather case and gazed out to sea. Then he looked at me appraisingly and asked:

"Do you know what Voodoo is?"

"I have a vague idea," I replied; "it's a negro cult, originating in Africa. Very ancient, I believe."

He began slowly filling his pipe, plainly dissatisfied with my sketchy answer.

"Voodoo isn't merely a cult," he spoke in little jerks between puffs at his pipe, "it's much more than that. It's a religion, a horrible, age-old religion. . . . Anyhow, if I'm going to tell you my story, I'd better hark back and start from the beginning."

Side by side we paced slowly backwards and forwards along the deck. The *Commewyne* was rolling gently; the only sound beside our voices was the sibilant washing of the waves as the ship cut through the swell. The silence seemed to convey to Sir Joshua some of the consuming curiosity that burned within me, for he suddenly started off again.

"To begin with, you must realize that Haiti is a sort of second home to me, for in my young days I was attached to our Embassy in Port-au-Prince. At that time the English ambassador there was Sir Spencer John, who probably knew as much about the history of the island as any living person. In order that you may clearly understand what I am going to tell you, I must go still farther back than that, because, in a curious way, the safe return of Columbus to the court of Queen Isabella was the indirect cause of my unfortunate experience.

"When Columbus returned to Spain, nothing could damp his enthusiasm for the new lands he had discovered, and the one that pleased him most was the tropical paradise he had named Hispaniola. The New Spain! For weeks on end he poured into the receptive ears of the Queen glowing accounts of the beautiful island, its kindly inhabitants, luxuriant vegetation, and, most wonderful of all, the gold which, so he declared, was to be had in unlimited quantities for the mere asking. It was this last consideration that drove hordes of greedy Spaniards westward as fast as their sails could carry them. On their arrival, the natives who till then had existed in a state of natural, simple contentment were set to work digging mines and opening up shafts. (These credulous adventurers had not taken long to discover that Columbus's story of gold lying about in heaps was very far from the truth.) Since the now unhappy islanders had had the good fortune to be born where all the necessities of life grew at their hut doors, they were physically incapable of any sort of heavy work, consequently they died off so quickly in the mines or at the hands of the Spaniards that they soon became extinct.

"The next development in the history of the island was its conquest by the French. When the French took possession of the land and settled down there, they soon found that there was an acute shortage of labor, so they conceived the cruel but ingenious idea of importing negroes from Africa and making them do the work to which the indigenous natives had succumbed.

Slave-hunters, fully equipped with loads of shackles and chains, penetrated into the interior of the Congo and the Gold Coast. Villages were surrounded, the useless niggers destroyed, and the strong or young put on one side as export goods to Haiti. Endless slave caravans wound their mournful way through the African bush. Blacks from Dahomey, Senegal, Sudan, and the Gold Coast trudged in endless columns down to the sea. Iron rings, clamped round their necks and strung on a long chain, made lagging impossible. None could drop out by the way. The dead and dying were dragged along by their fellows or occasionally galvanized into a semblance of life by the stinging lash of the overseer's whip. In this motley train, powerful bush-niggers strode beside youths of noble descent, full-grown women beside young girls, and beggars at the side of all-powerful medicine men. Over and amongst the caravans stalked the spirit of Voodoo.

"Transplanted to a new land, the old rites and orgies were recommenced in the virgin forests of Haiti. The curse of Voodoo covered the island.

"Although Voodoo flourishes in West Africa today as malignantly as it did a thousand years ago the origins and

Endless slave caravans wound their mournful way through the African bush

forms of this degrading religion are still shrouded in obscurity. What little we know is terrible enough.

"The priests are called 'Papaloi' by their followers, and the priestesses 'Mamaloi,' both words being Creole corruptions of 'Papa Roi' and 'Mama Roi.' (As you will discover, it is the custom among Haitians to address any revered person or animal as Papa and Mama. One frequently hears references to 'Papa Cochon,' 'Papa Boeuf,' or 'Mama Poule.')

"Besides practising a lot of abracadabra, the priests of Voodoo have an extraordinarily wide knowledge of medicines, especially of that branch relating to the properties of poisons; I believe the scientists call it toxicology. It is extremely dangerous to make an enemy of a priest, for besides a swift and simple death, he can deal in poisons that are both insidious and painful. With an apparently harmless drink he can produce raving insanity, delirium, slavering idiocy, impotence, paralysis, blindness, and even the living death of catalepsy. A wide range of weapons to have at one's command! Not the least of the qualifications which give the priests such absolute control over their people is their intimate acquaintance with the art of suggestion and hypnotism.

"Voodoo is the sublimated expression of the African mentality. The native believes that two souls inhabit the body; on his death the good soul returns to Africa to enjoy eternal happiness and bliss, while the evil soul hovers in the neighborhood of the corpse. In return for a small payment the priests undertake to exorcise these malignant spirits. . . ."

Higginbotham's concise explanations served to crystallize my conceptions of Voodoo which hitherto had been distinctly hazy. I knew now that I was talking to a man who was exceptionally well versed in this subject; indeed it was extraordinary to see how he was affected by his own recital. It seemed as if he had been suddenly recalled to an earlier existence, as though he himself moved in the shadow of this negro cult and wished me to share the experience. He beckoned to the steward who had just appeared on deck and told him to bring two easy chairs. We sat down and made ourselves comfortable.

"During my life in Haiti," he continued, "I've been through many weird experiences. Probably, if I were to relate half of them, you, in your Western superiority, would scoff at me. Anyway, I'll risk your skepticism and tell you one or two facts which any competent ethnologist will corroborate.

"The religious service of the Voodoo worshipers has developed in an unusual, not to say horrible way, caused almost entirely by the conditions of misery and oppression under which the negroes lived. You can well imagine what it must have been like on those stinking slave boats, where for weeks on end the closely packed bodies sweated and rotted under battened hatches. More than half died on the way. They were the lucky ones; for on the plantations the survivors were treated with indescribable brutality by their white masters. Only at dead of night could they gather together in the secret places of the forest and celebrate their ancient rituals. On these occasions the primitive instincts of the blacks were given free rein, and the monotonous rumble of the tom-toms inspired demoniacal dances, mad drinking orgies, and sexual frenzies. The priests knew, none better, how to make the fullest use of this uncontrollable urge for release and self-expression which possessed the downtrodden slaves. They organized nightly gatherings and debaucheries, and by this means established a terrible mastery throughout the whole of Haiti. With the massacre of the whites and the establishment of the black empire, Voodoo attained its zenith, and from that time on the land was under the absolute domination of the priests. Even the government acknowledged their power."

Higginbotham paused for a moment to refill his stumpy pipe. The heat from the sun at its height was becoming intense. I got up and removed my coat, and when I had settled down again, Sir Joshua stretched back in his chair and resumed his story.

"From out of these sexual orgies grew the atavistic impulse towards cannibalism. Definite feasts were instituted at which there was a ritual slaughter of children and even grown men, followed by a meal of roast flesh. These practices were carried to such extremes that when the American marines occupied the island a little while ago, many of the men who were unwise enough to wander off alone into the bush were later discovered murdered. The only relics found were a few scraped bones and some uniform buttons. The military records at Washington could reveal many such killings, committed solely for the sake of the ritual cooking-pot. And, what is more—this cannibalism is still going on today.

"You may wonder what all this has got to do with myself, but we have now arrived at the stage where Congo Bean Stew comes into the story. Perhaps you have already seen the connection? If not, I fear that at the end of my tale you will have but little appetite left for the excellent meal that is being prepared for us.

"The incidents which I am about to tell you took place during the reign of the black President, Fabre Geffrard, and at the time when I was stationed in Haiti. Some day I must tell you about President Geffrard; he was a great man and he was one of the few rulers of Haiti who recognized the full horror of Voodoo and fought against it with all his might."

From the ship's galley drifted an overpowering gust of roasting pork which mingled unpleasantly with the hot and oily air arising out of the engine room. Except for the flavor of his tobacco, Sir Joshua seemed unconscious of his surroundings and he continued sucking away noisily at his pipe.

"In two days," he said, "we shall be landing in the capital of Haiti, Port-au-Prince. Only a few miles from there lies the little negro village of Bizóton, where, at the time of my story, there lived a Mamaloi by the name of Jeanne Pelle, together with her brother, Congo Pelle. A great Voodoo festival had been announced and these two made arrangements for a child-sacrifice. The victim finally decided upon was Jeanne's little twelve-year-old niece, Claircine, who was carried off into the jungle and kept a prisoner in the temple until the time arrived. It is unnecessary to go into details about what actually happened. On the great night there was a large assembly of worshipers. The priests cut the child's throat and drank the blood according to ritual, and with the flesh they cooked a Congo Bean Stew; for, according to Haitian connoisseurs, human meat tastes best when boiled with Congo beans. The negroes were delighted with the dish, and the night finished up with the customary wild dances and licentious sexual performances. . . ."

There followed a long pause while my companion remained deep in thought. Then he cleared his throat and went on:

"Since the devotees had the audacity to hold their cannibal feast within practically a stone's throw of the capital, it was impossible to prevent the anti-Voodoo authorities from getting wind of the affair. They quickly discovered the eight ringleaders, arrested them, and tried them on a charge of murder."

The sickly smell of the pork seemed to disturb Sir Joshua, for he got up and leant over the rail, gazing down at the water. Then he knocked out his pipe and stuffed it into his pocket. At that moment the lunch gong sounded and I made a motion to get up. He laid a hand on my shoulder and smiled.

"I've nearly finished now, so listen for a few minutes longer.

"My active dislike of Congo Bean Stew dates from the day of the trial. I had to go with Sir Spencer John to the proceedings because he was writing a book on Haiti, and wanted to get some first-hand information about this aspect of Voodoo. We were given a seat right in the front of the courthouse, beside a table on which were laid out the gruesome relics of the feast. There were some bones, scraped quite clean; a skull in the same condition, and the sacrificial knives. Just at my right elbow was the most disgusting exhibit of the lot. It was a large soup bowl containing the remains of the stew. It looked just like Lancashire hot-pot, only the pieces of meat embedded in the congealed fat were *human flesh*. As things were, I wasn't feeling at my best that morning, but the sight of the bowl and its horrible contents compelled me to hurry outside. I just managed to get round the corner before I was sick. When I was able to raise my head again, I found the Spanish ambassador beside me. Don Mariano Alvarez had also been seized with an uncontrollable nausea. When we had sufficiently recovered we went inside again. It was only with the greatest physical effort that I managed to last out the trial and hear the judges condemn all the prisoners to death.

"On the day of the execution the President had to turn out the whole garrison to guard against disturbances. In the souvenir shops today one can still buy picture postcards of the turmoil and the firing party. After the volley there arose a menacing shout from the crowd and the last words of the dead priests went round from mouth to mouth: 'They may shoot us, but in the night we will rise from our graves.' The next morning, in spite of a careful watch, the bodies had vanished and in their coffins were found the carcasses of goats. This is the absolute truth, and anyone who was in Port-au-Prince at the time will tell you the same. What really happened to the corpses I never discovered; perhaps they were cooked up into another Congo Bean Stew! So perhaps you understand now why I can't bear even the smell of the stuff."

We both got up and strolled a few times round the deck to get a little fresh air. In front of us a scarlet butterfly hovered like a lambent flame over one of the hatches.

When we reached the bar, we both entered as if by tacit consent. "Two double Scotch," ordered Higginbotham, "to give us an appetite for luncheon."

We drank four for safety.

Five a.m.

The anchor fell into the water with a loud splash and rattle. The ship blew off steam and let out a little more chain. Then followed three short blasts from the siren and the S.S. *Commewyne* lay at anchor, rocking gently on the bay of Cap Haitien.

Before us curved the gleaming coral beach under the shadow of the leaning palms. Around the town lay wide sloping fields of sugar cane, and beyond, rising up to the foothills, stretched the impenetrable forest.

Above all, dominating the entire landscape, towered a giant range of rugged mountains, scarred with bottomless ravines and gorges absorbing the sun and throwing back no light.

Involuntarily my thoughts strayed back to the dark, dramatic days of the past when the slaves of Haiti burst their shackles and turned on their white oppressors. In this quiet village which lay before me a fanatical horde, drunk with the taste of blood, had danced to the ancient, mad refrain which throbbed from the drums of human skin. Slave-generals in tri-cornered hats, braided uniforms, scarlet sashes, and thigh boots, had fought their way through intrigue and murder to riches, power, and glory. What a strange story that had been. . . .

The sun which by now had risen above the edge of the Caribbean threw its first clear rays over this tropical creation, this crumbling garden of paradise and hell. A large brown pelican, head drawn back, grotesque beak projecting, skimmed over the sea in search of breakfast. He dived swiftly, reappeared immediately, and flew away with a struggling fish in his beak.

The distant mountains glowed coppery-red above the pellucid blue of the sea; the mists of night still wreathed their summits. Slowly the clouds divided and, far inland, below the precipitous peaks of the giant Bonnet l'Evêque, a lofty plateau appeared whose edges fell perpendicularly into the sea.

The clouds rolled down again.

In that brief moment I had glimpsed the mightiest edifice ever created by the hand of Man in either of the two Americas. A monumental colossus, as large as the pyramids of Gizeh, as beautiful as Windsor Castle, as inaccessible as the Potala in Lhasa. It was the incarnation of the dreams of a negro king, whose dramatic life, meteoric rise to fame, and equally sudden eclipse, can scarcely have had an equal in the history of the world.

I had seen La Ferrière, the citadel of King Christophe.

. . . .

A church bell rang out. Dogs barked and the braying of mules competed with the harsh call of a rooster. A pungent smell of burning wood drifted across the water. The village was visibly waking to life. Now a broad-beamed boat shot out from the shore with a dozen half-naked negroes pulling at the oars. At the stern fluttered the blue and red flag of the Republic, while huddled together amidships was a motley assortment of black officers, American marines, and natives, all smoking cigarettes. Other boats put off from the jetty, filled with laughing, chattering blacks who soon clustered round our ship, displaying their varied merchandise of pineapples, aguas, mangoes, alligator pears, and bananas. These were held up for our inspection, together with huge glittering mussels and brightly hued parrots, while affectionate little monkeys ran about over the heads of the natives. All around us was a mass of black, woolly heads, white rolling eyes, and ivory teeth. In time-honored custom the naked youths dived into the water and fetched up the coins we threw to them. . . .

Being the only passenger who was leaving the ship here, there was a sharp tussle among the natives as to who should have the privilege of rowing me ashore. I managed at last to collect all my baggage on one boat and we started off. The moving dots on the shore which I had seen from the ship quickly resolved themselves at our approach into mules and dogs and gesticulating men. The landing stage, a decaying structure half under water, was of little use to us and, since it was low tide, the boat grounded a good hundred yards from dry land. The boatmen took my boxes and painting equipment on their heads and waded ashore, leaving me to the mercies of an undersized little fellow who indicated to me that I was to climb on his back. I obediently straddled my two-legged horse and rode safely to the beach, landing on the ruins of an ancient concrete gun-embrasure.

So this was Haiti!

II.
IN CARIBBEAN WATERS

My stay in Cap Haitien was not destined to be a long one. I wandered round the town for a while and eventually ended up at the harbor. Amongst the shipping there I noticed a picturesque boat with patched, multicolored sails and the most villainous-looking crew I had ever set eyes on. Painted on the stern of the boat was an inscription which I managed to decipher after some effort:

Santa Rita
Guantanamo, Cuba.

Directly above flapped a sun-bleached, tattered rag, once evidently the proud flag of the "Pearl of the Antilles" as Cuba calls itself.

In response to my question the solitary Haitian customs officer informed me that the schooner *Santa Rita* was bound for Santo Domingo, calling in on its way at the tiny ports that fringe the north coast of Haiti.

This fitted in with my plans perfectly for I wanted to see the real Haiti from an unconventional angle. José Perez, the owner and captain of the *Santa Rita*, was drinking with a group of mulattoes in one of the waterside cafés and, apparently, at the same time keeping one eye vigilant on the loading of his ship. I introduced myself to him and, finding him extremely affable, suggested what I had in mind. After a few drinks we managed to strike a bargain. In return for my standing one more round of rum and painting a portrait of him, Perez undertook to transport me and my baggage to the next port of call, Fort Liberté, on the frontier of Santo Domingo.

A little after midnight the *Santa Rita* raised anchor. The scattered houses of Cap Haitien and the plume of white smoke from the sugar mill soon vanished into the distance. The ragged outline of the mountains, darker against the dark sky beyond, sank low on the horizon. I turned into the cabin that had been allotted to me and, after a few twistings and turnings, lay comfortably in my hammock. Sleep soon came, induced by the gentle motion of the boat.

The next morning I woke late and walked out on deck to find the sun blazing down from a scorching cloudless sky. The heat was intolerable, sapping all energy, mental and physical, and making the very act of breathing an effort. Soon it would be impossible to think! I hung over the rail and gazed at the water as if by contemplating the heavy peacock blue I might gain some respite from the heat. The schooner slipped through the water, leaving in its wake a gently hissing

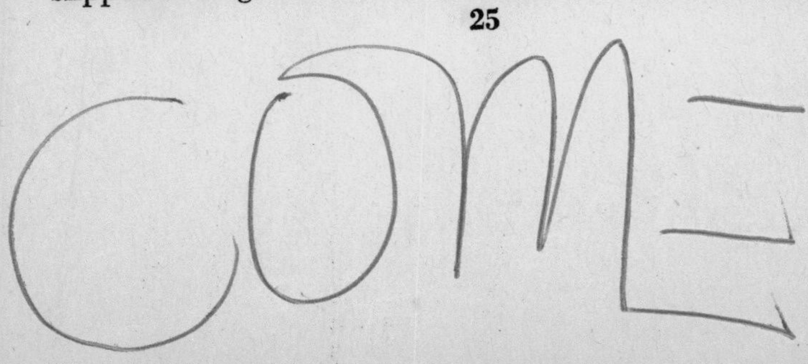

stream that lulled the senses. The sun, the sea, and the sky were fused into one great blue incandescent bowl. And I felt that I too was ablaze with them. In the torrid heat the ropes hung down like dried-up snakes, and the sails bellied out, loose and heavy as ill-hung curtains. The slightest touch of bare flesh on the iron rails raised a blister.

From bow to stern a long sail had been stretched across the deck as a protection from the sun, and the murmur of voices and momentary laughter indicated the presence of other human beings besides myself in this infernal melting-pot. I slung my hammock from the mast where there seemed to be the faintest traces of a draught and, from my vantage point, I took leisurely note of the mixed crowd beneath the awning.

From the artistic point of view Captain José Perez was a fascinating fellow, large and strong featured, of the southern type (probably a Cuban), his sparse hair brushed straight back and plastered down like a black satin skull-cap on his head. Round his waist he had wound a scarlet sash. His feet were thrust into a pair of slippers which had obviously been cut down from shoes far too big for him, for he had great difficulty in keeping them on and was forced to walk about the deck with little flip-flap steps. A long stride might have lost them overboard! In contrast to his great virility there was something decidedly feminine about him, an impression that was greatly heightened by a large gold ear-ring, the size of a shilling, which hung down from his left ear.

A negro stood at the wheel, gazing dreamily into the distance. The spokes ran through his fingers, first one way and then the other, without seeming to make any impression on the course of the ship. Directly in front of me, and with movements so slow that each one was etched against the deck, sat a negro mending a net.

All at once the ship woke to life. A giggling and chattering that reminded me of a girls' school on their Sunday outing rose from the saloon below. A troupe of young mulattoes rushed up the companion-way and chased one another across the deck. They were a fine lot of boys, their skins a delicate coffee color, their bodies slim and beautifully modeled and proportioned. They were dressed in white shirts and trousers, the latter being very tight about the upper parts and wide at the bottom after the Mexican style.

But their faces! Powdered to a startling whiteness from which stood out a pair of black-rimmed, soft brown eyes and unnaturally strawberry-red lips. A queer crowd! They huddled together on one side of the deck like a brood of young cuckoos and conversed in a high-pitched falsetto which reminded me of the frantic twittering of birds. Some of them leant over the rails and made faces at their reflections in the water, or, alternatively, admired each other. The latter seemed more to their liking. . . .

At meal times we all ate together at a long table set in the stern of the ship. Amongst this ruffianly crew there were naturally no table manners and everyone stretched across to snatch at the choicest morsels in the dish. The food was worse than indifferent. Most of the potatoes were sour, as was the bread, and the tinned Danish butter never failed to appear in the form of a thin yellow liquid. The meat was also of the tinned variety and was often served in a sauce of unknown, and therefore unspeakable, ingredients. The cook had evidently no mind for subterfuge, for the leathery portions that one day were concealed beneath little segments of pie crust were served up the following day on a tin plate as unadorned "meat." At the best of times eating was more of a duty than a pleasure; the only things that I consumed with relish were the bananas and other tropical fruit, which could not have much wrong with them. The tepid drinking water was made palatable by an admixture of lime-juice and Jamaica rum. At any rate this beverage produced a happy feeling of friendliness and helped us largely to forget the grilling heat.

One day, according to our agreement, I made a hasty sketch of the captain which, when finished, seemed to please him inordinately. He vanished with it (flip-flap) into his cabin. My straining ears caught sounds of furniture being moved about and a moment later a crumpled ball of paper flew out of the window and fell into the sea.

So much for my *magnum opus!* I thought wryly.

I hurried into the cabin.

There, over the captain's bed, hung my sketch, pinned into a monstrous gold frame from which he had just torn out the portrait of the President of Cuba!

So far, in spite of the heat, a steady progress had been maintained, but now that more than half of the journey was completed, we ran into a sudden calm. If the air had been oppressive, hot, and enervating before, it was ten times more so now. The flaccid sails hung on the mast, the coast remained its unvarying distance, and the ship drifted in a glassy sea where there were no wavelets to slap against the bow, no wake of foam, no perceptible motion. We were just waiting.

Owing to its clarity the water looked like an aquarium, no more than a fathom in depth. It was a wonderful sight. Against a backcloth of shining silver sand moved brightly colored star-fish, sea-urchins, and many other tiny denizens of underwater life; glittering with every imaginable hue and color, fiery red, emerald green, deepest blue, dazzling saffron, all swimming this way and that in an ever-moving, natural kaleidoscope. Forests of sea plants, corals, anemone, flabella, and grotesque sponges waved their delicate fronds in the water. The whole incredibly beautiful submarine garden swayed lightly in the currents like fields of tropical flowers; it seemed that one could pluck the blooms by merely stretching out a hand. I tried and found I was deceived—the sea bed was not within reach of a three-yard pole.

There were also hundreds of molluscs with exquisite gradations of color, some of the loveliest of which a pretty mulatto lad fished out of the sea in a pail. Alas—they began to die immediately. The rainbow hues faded away, leaving only drab and faded shell-fish. We threw them back into the water as quickly as possible, where slowly all their former beauty returned to them. Madrepores lay on the sandbanks, some shaped like shovels, some like snakes. One, with the most beautiful tracery, I fished out with a hook and line. Directly it reached the air it fell to dust.

The currents carried the *Santa Rita* over broad coral banks of deepest red. Seen from above the curious shapes suggested a submerged city, an underwater Venice with miniature castles, bridges, houses, and leafless trees. Brightly scaled fishes hovered motionless in line over the tiny city like a fierce aërial horde; then they made a sudden swirl and disappeared. At my request the captain produced a long pole to which I tied about twenty yards of string with a hook on the end. I impaled a chunk of tinned meat on the barb and trailed it in the water. The fishes could be clearly seen swimming after the bait, and soon a shoal of little ones came along and nibbled it all away. I pulled the line in and the negro at the wheel stuck another bit of bait on, winding it round with a piece of white cloth so that only a tiny end of the meat was visible. This time the little fishes nibbled in vain. Suddenly they scattered, making way for an absolute monarch of the deep. This monster took the bait in one gulp and dashed off—to the end of the slack. With great presence of mind I had dropped the pole and caught hold of the line, so that when the fish came to the end of his tether he was pulled up short instead of, as he had obviously hoped, breaking the pole. He met this resistance by threshing the water to a cloud of spray, but he did not otherwise put up much of a fight and I began drawing him slowly in. I thought triumphantly, "My first shark! How easy!" He was soon out of the water, his scales glittering with all the colors of the spectrum.

My pride suffered a disappointment for it was no shark, but a dolphin, with his peculiar turned-up mouth which enables him to chase flying fish until they become exhausted and fall into his gaping jaws. Once on the deck he put up a valiant fight with his captors, twisting to and fro in his convulsions, while his metallic scales glowed like a captive rainbow, as if fired anew by fresh reserves of strength. First he shone like a lump of pure gold, quickly changing to turquoise blue, and immediately after glittering green. Then came an incomparable magenta, dissolving at last into a dirty brown. The fish lay dead—the fire was quenched. Well, we would eat him for dinner! It seemed like vandalism, but we were told that he would make a meal fit for a king.

After this excitement we were preparing to kick our heels for another spell of boredom when, inexplicably, a light breeze sprang up and we bowled along at a brisk pace towards our destination. The coast line came nearer, gradually strengthening its contours and outline like the developing of a photographic negative. Villages became visible and soon I could distinguish individual dwellings and the low palm-fringed shore. Clearly across the water came the sounds of life, the lowing of cattle and the shouts of native fishermen. We would be in harbor soon.

The breeze, however, was fickle. As inexplicably as before, the wind changed again and blew almost at gale force away from land. The captain spat out a fierce oath mingled with a brown stream of tobacco juice. The anchor fell rattling to the bottom and the clear water muddied with swirling sand. There we hove to, only a few miles from Fort Liberté. . . .

A flotilla of small fishing boats put out from shore and took up positions a short distance off. The occupants then commenced to fish. Their methods were elementary in the extreme, but, it must be admitted, extraordinarily effective. The boats formed a rough rectangle and a vast net was lowered in the middle of them. Then the negroes commenced a weird and heathen performance, yelling like lunatics and beating the water with their oars. The din was enough to rouse the dead, not to speak of the fishes who fled in every direction. At this crucial moment the net was hauled up, chock full of fish, and the contents were emptied into the boats. Little fish were thrown back into the sea, the larger ones bundled into casks, and the giants were killed immediately since their writhings and flappings threatened to upset the little cockleshell boats.

On the *Santa Rita* all was peaceful in the noonday heat. The crew had returned to their siesta which had been so rudely disturbed by my dolphin and the ensuing breeze. I, too, crept under the protective sail. . . .

It was seven o'clock when I awoke. The sky was ablaze with that penultimate radiance that precedes the setting of the sun, a radiance whose exotic colors are never seen elsewhere than in the tropics. Against an indigo background were dark streaks of cloud through which pierced spear-like rays of burning gold. On deck the day-time canopy had been taken down, there was no need for it now in the cool of the evening. Slowly the sun sank below the waves and soon a million stars were twinkling above me. The landward silhouettes awoke to life in gleaming pin-points of light, mountain fires whose smoke wavered in the wind, ghostly gray against the black peaks beyond. From the jungle of the hinterland throbbed the deep message of a tom-tom. Beneath us the sea rustled along the hull of the ship; above a sail flapped, a mast creaked under the strain of a gust of wind, a rope chafed at the added weight. It was a night of mystery, of desire, and of an intense tropical harmony.

Like shadows the sailors slipped by. Real life began for them at nightfall. In a corner a group of negroes squatted on deck with closed eyes and hummed an old plantation spiritual, gently swaying their bodies in rhythm to the tune. Overhead a solitary ship's lantern swung and threw transient shadows over the group. . . .

After supper one of the sailors fetched a concertina, another produced a guitar, and the two of them improvised as a dance band. In sharp accents a Cuban rumba rang out and the audience accompanied the tune by clapping their hands in time. One of the mulatto boys stepped into the circle and danced. I had never seen a Cuban rumba danced before, but my impression was that it was some sort of ballroom step. I was mistaken. Never in my life had I seen such a performance, and I never thought anything could exceed its wildness and licentiousness until I saw a negress dance the native rumba a few months later. The boy began with slow suggestive movements which gradually grew quicker until at last he was flinging his legs around in apparently double-jointed frenzy and jerking his body to and fro, while he thrashed the air with his arms. Faster and faster grew the music and the boy whirled round with still increasing speed. When it seemed that he must do himself some frightful injury, the music stopped, suddenly, on a crashing chord. The finale was greeted with tremendous applause.

Now the musicians set up a slower dance tune and couples started revolving on the deck. Captain, mate, and sailor, each took a mulatto boy as partner and shuffled round to the best of his ability. One dance followed another and the fun became fast and furious. Only when the musicians wearied of their impromptu performance did the ship lie quiet again.

I leant for a while over the rail studying the stars. As I returned to my hammock half-an-hour later, I peeped into the captain's cabin. Tightly clasped together they slept there blissfully, the head of each resting on the other's shoulder: Captain Perez and a mulatto boy.

When I woke up the next morning an unaccustomed silence pervaded the schooner. Usually at this hour there would be a chatter of voices and much running to and fro. What was amiss? I looked out of the porthole and saw with surprise that the *Santa Rita* was no longer at sea, but lying in a lovely sheltered lagoon, tied up to a wooden pier. A little way off lay a tiny village of palm-thatched roofs and white walls with a crumbling church tower in the background.

We had arrived at Fort Liberté. At the time of the French colonization this settlement had been called "Fort Dauphin," a name later changed by King Christophe to "Fort Royal." After Christophe's fall the place had lain desolate and forgotten for almost a century. Then it had been repopulated and had received its present high-sounding appellation.

Here I took my farewell of the *Santa Rita* and her picturesque crew. Captain Perez did me the honor to wake up from his siesta in order to see me off the ship. He embraced me in true Spanish fashion. Unfortunately I was unable to prevent him planting two alcoholic kisses on my cheeks before he bade me a final *adiós*. Then I stepped ashore.

I arranged for my luggage to be left on the quay to be collected later and walked up to the market place. On one side of the square was the church, whose tumble-down appearance I had already noted from the boat. It was a bleached and collapsing structure, overgrown with fig trees and creeping plants which sprouted lavishly from every nook and cranny. Opposite the church was a primitive ox-cart with huge, irregular wooden-disc wheels almost obscuring a tin-roofed bungalow over whose porch waved the national flag of Haiti. Immediately above the doorway hung a notice-board painted with a peeling coat of arms and the words:

GENDARMERIE D'HAITI

Even in black Haiti it is a good plan to be on the best of terms with the officials, so I therefore decided to introduce myself to the commandant. Expectantly I climbed the creaking steps which led to the veranda of the "fort." Eight strapping fellows in khaki uniform lounged on a bench against the wall. On my appearance they sprang to attention with a single "crack!" and saluted. The corporal strode out of the building and reported that his "garrison of eight men stood at my command." In a flash I saw what had happened. On account of my khaki shirt and shorts I had been mistaken for an inspecting officer. At the same moment I realized that unless I wished to injure the negroes' extremely sensitive and susceptible nature, I must be careful to meet the ludicrous situation with all seriousness. I therefore expressed my thanks and approval with such condescension as I thought befitted an exalted general and left the bungalow with all haste. Behind me eight rifle-butts crashed on the planking, raising a choking cloud of dust from the cracks. . . .

The grass-grown high street led to a building which possessed the exalted name, "Grand Hôtel de Paris." It was a dreary, one-storied shack, shunned, as I learnt afterwards, by the natives and visited only by strangers, who went there perforce, since Fort Liberté boasted no other accommodation.

Against one side of the building leaned a flourishing pair of orange trees, evidently bent on toppling the crooked and crumbling walls to final destruction.

I pushed open the front door and walked into the living room. Through the half-light of the interior the first thing that caught my eyes was a tier of shelves on which reposed rows of bottles flaunting the proud labels of the best European distilleries. A thick layer of dust and cobwebs proved conclusively that none of the bottles had been needed for a very considerable time.

I thought at first that the room was empty and I rattled a near-by chair. The figure of an obese but kindly looking negress rose up from behind the bar and introduced herself to me as Madame Vaublanc, my hostess. My entrance had evidently disturbed her contemplations but she showed no annoyance for she was an amiable old soul. She usually sat behind the bar and dozed, pleased with herself and her lot, wanting nothing, unmoved by the world outside. Should a guest stray into the hotel by mistake, she was instantly on the alert, bustling about with food and drinks. But should no one come, and this was the usual rule, well—no one came, and Madame, still content with her fate, could sit and dream the whole day long.

Today was the great exception, she had a white visitor. This happened so seldom that Madame had to collect herself mentally before she could supply me with any information. After this short but necessary delay her tongue raced on like a river in spate. Her food was the best and tastiest in the whole republic (here she threw me a meaning glance) . . . her rooms were the coolest on the island . . . there were no cleaner, pleasanter, nor softer beds in Haiti . . . and finally, was not Madame Vaublanc's hospitality renowned from Bahia

Blanca to Bermuda? . . . At this last statement she had the grace to blush, her black complexion turning a strange mottled color.

"Or if the gentleman likes a little company—something pale brown from Santo Domingo?—the creole girls from Santo Domingo are world-famous, just the right mixture of Spanish nobility, Caribbean contours and African passion . . . quien sabe?"

I stemmed her flow of suggestions and said, "No, thank you. Not at the moment. All I want now is a bath."

"*Oui, monsieur. Certainement, monsieur.* The bathroom is on the first floor, just next to the guest-room. Mademoiselle Justine! Mademoiselle Juuu—stiiiine!! *Conduisez ce monsieur à sa chambre.*"

Justine, the black kitchenmaid and chambermaid combined, appeared from the back yard and led me upstairs to the bathroom. I quickly started to undress and was nearly ready to get into the bath when I happened to look round, and there was Justine leaning against the door, watching me with interest. She seemed to find nothing extraordinary in keeping me company when I bathed and it took me several minutes to convince her that this was an exhibition that concerned only myself and the four walls; a larger audience I would not allow. When she finally disappeared, her face blank with disappointment, I looked round for the bath. It was nowhere to be seen. The only articles in the room were a large tub, a pail of water reposing on a stool, and a little iron basin. It did not require much intelligence to guess the method of operation, for the little iron basin on the floor gave the clue to the whole procedure. I had to stand in the tub and ladle the tepid water over myself. Such is the evil method of bathing in Haiti.

After my bath I dressed again and went out onto the veranda to rest. I settled in a comfortable wicker chair. With a sense of pleasant contentment I filled my pipe with black Haitian tobacco and commenced to study the scene that lay before me.

The sun had sunk behind a clump of banana trees whose long flat leaves stood silhouetted blackly against the crimson glow. A gentle grass-grown slope led down to the water front, dotted with fruit-laden orange and lemon trees. Between them shone jeweled glimpses of the deep blue sea. The air was vibrant with the usual noises of a tropical evening. Mosquitoes hummed, grasshoppers trilled, frogs croaked in a distant and not unpleasant symphony. Later on, when I was camping in the forest, I found this nocturnal cacophony far from soothing. But now it was definitely pleasant, improving the taste of my tobacco and my drink, a soft accompaniment to the fading sunset. The evening breeze carried the sweet scent of ripening fruit across verdant lawns. . . .

Two negro girls strolled slowly along the road below and gazed at the white stranger with ogling curiosity. Coquettishly they let the tops of their dresses slip down from their shoulders showing beautiful black satiny bodies. Whenever my glance caught theirs, they smiled with happiness and amusement. Then they laughed out loud and executed a little dance, bending and swaying their bodies enticingly. When this performance was over they turned round and walked back to their huts, every now and then turning their heads to look back at me with open invitation.

The day was nearly over.

The palm trees grew hazy and indistinct. The moon rose slowly, casting its flat silver sheen over the landscape. Above the trees twinkled the Southern Cross. In the dark bushes

The day was nearly over

fireflies came to life. Some birds flew to their nesting places uttering plaintive cries. The village, undisturbed by their noise, lay like a painted picture spread before me.

The local dandies, clad in white trousers and red flowing ties, entered the scene and stole along shady paths to the huts of their waiting demoiselles.

It was late.

The streets were now quite empty. Flickering oil lamps that all the evening had been burning on the street corners were now extinguished. From a near-by hut arose a burst of suppressed laughter, from another came the twanging of a guitar. Against a corner a soldier leaned, yawning widely as he balanced his rifle on his shoulder like a lance poised to throw.

From the thick undergrowth at the end of the road came the thousand-voiced barking call of the bullfrogs and the harsh cries of parrots, while far beyond—out in the jungle where all paths end—sounded the hoarse grunting of the sluggish alligators. The noises died away.

Large and bright stood the full moon above the horizon. The sea, glittering like mother-of-pearl, lapped softly against the beach. All else was still.

The air was motionless; the village lay breathing silently.

A chill breath swept among the trees, rustling the leaves.

The *Santa Rita* now laden with bananas left her moorings and glided soundlessly out to the open sea. Her port and starboard lights reflected red and green in the water.

The beach lay solitary and deserted. Under the brilliant radiance of the moon each separate pebble glistened on the sand where the waves had retreated and left a shining wetness.

Fort Liberté, cradled between the mountains and the sea, slept. . . .

III. MASSACRE RIVER

FOUR HUNDRED YEARS ago the Caribbeans were unknown to the civilized world and they might very well have remained in the same condition for several centuries to come had not two very natural and unavoidable causes contributed to their discovery. Firstly, an island whose native name was Quisqueya, lay directly in the path of Columbus's vaguely wandering fleet. This disability need not have been serious, for had the island presented no special attractions beyond its ordinary tropical luxuriance, Columbus would probably have sailed on in search of a richer and more productive country. But here the natives made their second and unwitting mistake. They allowed their naked babies to play in the dirty puddles—and their playthings were balls of gold.

So the Spaniards had come to stay.

The ignorant natives were not averse to exchanging their children's toys for glass balls, and, when that commodity gave out, for lead balls. Both parties profited by this exchange, at least so the natives thought; but then they could not know that Spain was a large country and had many ships.

Other adventurers followed in the wake of Columbus, and one day there sailed into the bay where Fort Liberté now stands a wonderful and stately armada—brightly beflagged, richly decorated—the great and noble galleons of Spain. The commander of the fleet, round-bellied Cortez, had not come there by chance. He had heard, from some doubtless authentic source, that the river Guatapano, which emptied into the bay, was said to wash down quantities of gold silt from a mountain of solid gold somewhere in the interior. So he had come to investigate the rumor. But he himself had another and more important project on hand, the conquest of Mexico, so to his boon companion in fighting and drinking, Don Pedro Hermanos Granados, he entrusted the task of exploring the river, discovering the legendary mountain of gold, and taking possession of it in the name of Cortez and the king of Spain.

Granados was only too pleased to undertake what seemed to him to be an easy and possibly lucrative expedition. Just before he left for Manzanillo Bay, he fired a farewell salvo to which Cortez' fleet replied. Then his galleon vanished round the bend. From that moment on no trace of the ship was ever seen again. No more was ever heard of Don Pedro Hermanos Granados and his crew of hardened conquistadores.

I heard this story from a knowledgeable native in Fort

Then his galleon vanished round the bend

Liberté and I decided to try and follow in the tracks of the mysterious Granados. Admittedly I had no galleon at my disposal, but a fair-sized rowboat was sufficient, and certainly far more suitable, for my purpose.

In the harbor below I discovered and bought from a fisherman a roomy but primitive boat, which, judging from its broad beam, had not been built for speed. I hopefully christened her *Brush-by* and painted the name large and legibly on both sides of the bow. Without much difficulty I stepped a mast and attached to it a bast sail. Having made these simple preparations, I announced that I was looking for a crew. As a result of this appeal the whole of the youth of Fort Liberté besieged me, clamoring to be engaged; I could have filled a training ship with the crowd that collected. After much arguing and shouting I chose the six sturdiest looking lads that I could see, and they promptly declared themselves willing to enter my service for the price of one gourde a day (about twenty cents) and food, adding as an extra inducement that they would accompany me to the end of the world—or at any rate to the end of the island. Their names were as strange as their appearance: Rauri—Ottavio—Kanka—Ford—Bonaparte, and a sixth whose name was incomprehensible to me, consisting of negroid syllables which could never be expressed in the Latin alphabet. I called him Granados and he was pleased with it. Ford had only just got his name; he had been knocked down a week earlier by a Ford car which had run amok, and, as a reminder of this privilege, he had borne from then on the name of the car from Detroit. In order to avoid confusion I wrote each boy's name in ink across the front of his trousers; a vain precaution, for after a few weeks' wear the whole garment had turned the same color as the ink.

We spent the afternoon stowing our baggage, tent, and tinned food aboard, and finally hoisted sail at midnight. The whole population of the town, including the garrison of eight men and a corporal, came to see us go. My leave-taking with Madame Vaublanc was touching in the extreme. She was sorry to see her white visitor depart and she showed her unhappiness by presenting me with a large bottle of rum and weeping copiously. Then I stepped aboard and we cast off.

The wind drove us swiftly along the coast of Haiti and by sunrise we found ourselves in Manzanillo Bay, at the eastern extremity of the Black Republic. The bay was wide and turgid with the muddy waters of the Massacre River which debouched into the center of its sweep. We sailed along close inshore, and as we approached the mouth we had to thread our way between long, low sandy islands which formed an intricate delta to the river. On these islands the only vegetation was a few hardy trees, which grew smooth and bleached by the flood-waters, sticking out of the bare soil like the ribs of primeval mastodons. There were no signs of habitation anywhere on the islands along the shore of the bay.

On one of these numerous islands, the Isleta de Caimana, I saw my first alligators. Even before we rounded the point which brought them into view, I knew that something unusual lay there by the powerful and unpleasant smell of musk which filled the air. There they were, two huge saurians, lying like stranded logs half in and half out of the water. Their jaws gaped lazily; possibly even they were suffering from the hot, moist atmosphere that made every breath a weary effort. Some birds rather like starlings were picking maggots and insects from the scaly backs of the monsters, while one cheeky little fellow made himself useful as a toothpick, snatching his food from between the alligator's teeth. Only the black, malignant little eyes showed that there was still life in the animals. As we got nearer, I raised my revolver and fired. For a moment nothing happened, then one of the alligators slithered into the muddy water and sank out of sight, only the bubbles bursting on the surface showed his hiding place. The other withdrew stolidly into the slime.

I had chosen a bad time for my expedition. The rainy season was nearing its end and, as a result, the banks of the river were so flooded that no land was to be seen, just the trunks of the trees growing up out of the water. The flooding was evidently not more than a foot deep, for on the banks, or rather where the banks should have been, were numbers of cranes and flamingoes, pensively poised on one leg.

We had been paddling up the river for a short while when it suddenly began to narrow. The banks of dense jungle closed in on us until the sky above seemed almost as near as the water below. It was a curious sensation, like being at the bottom of a well shaft or a deep canyon. A dragonfly came out of the undergrowth and hovered over the boat, its rainbow wings shimmering in the sunlight. Then it darted off in a flash of prismatic light. No one spoke. The oars creaked in the rowlocks and the splashing of water echoed between the dark walls of the forest. I sat in the stern steering with a long oar and silently cursing the moist heat which made each movement an agony, when the slightest motion brought sweat starting out from every pore in one's body.

The silence of the forest where not a leaf stirred grew as oppressive as the heat. The boys felt this too and began shouting to one another. But after each echo died away, the stillness that fell only served as a greater emphasis of our loneliness. Now and again the boat shot under low-hanging branches and we all had to duck quickly to avoid the boughs and leaves that brushed across our backs. Under their shadow the cool and darkness was a pleasant respite from the direct heat of the sun, but the natives always seemed to be happier when we emerged into the open river which they greeted with more shouting and laughter.

I had long given up hope of ever reaching human habitation before nightfall when suddenly I rubbed my eyes in amazement. Surely that was a mirage: the low straw roofs of negro huts nestling behind the trees. As we approached nearer the huts grew more distinct. It was no mirage but a small native village. Chocolate-colored babies sat on the bank and amongst them pranced haughty stork-like birds who seemed to be awaiting only my arrival and instructions in order to pick out a selected baby and deliver it to any given address.

On our arrival in Embochure, as the village was called, the inhabitants all came out of their huts and goggled at us as though we had just fallen from the skies. However, they soon became friendly and after a short palaver with my crew agreed to provide us with some habitable lodgings. I preferred to sleep in the open, for these people live in a state of unbelievable dirt and indigence; they make no demands of life and life makes none of them.

Evening was falling and before the swift tropical twilight had quite died away a large fire had been built, on which were thrown green tobacco leaves whose aromatic smoke kept the swarms of troublesome mosquitoes at bay. We had some supper and then tried to get what sleep we could.

The next morning we packed up at dawn and started up the river again. From a passing sandbank came the powerful sickly stench of corruption. The oarsmen pulled faster as we passed and I saw the decaying body of an alligator creeping with millions of maggots. The scenery bordering the river was not exactly what one would expect in a tropical paradise. There was a certain monotony about the forest as seen from the river which conjured up the picture of a façade of big city tenements on a gloomy winter's afternoon. Since time immemorial the forest had served as the burial place of fallen, rotting leaves, from whose morass the high tree trunks soared like the pillars in a cathedral, spreading at the top into a dense roof of foliage which effectively shut out any ray of sunshine from the eternal twilight below.

Thousands of swinging lianas knotted these forest giants into a vast unity. Each tree had its own parasites to nourish, and many were so overladen by the throttling embrace that all light and air was cut off from them and they themselves died in the struggle. Mighty roots writhed out of the earth and down to the river like streams of solid lava. Clumps of bamboos glided by. From the distance they looked colorless and drab, but on closer approach their appearance changed completely. There stood revealed a fine mosaic of delicate pink and yellow mosses growing on the supple stems.

On either bank the dense jungle stood dark and secretive. Now and again it was lit up by a fugitive gleam of sunlight. Whenever this happened I saw a cool vista of delicate green ferns and pointed palms, but apart from these short interludes the journey was as uneventful as the day before. No signs of life, no sounds—only the sweltering heat. As the sun sank behind the woods, the lower trunks were already in thick darkness while the last blazing radiance lit the treetops in a bright green glow. A light breeze sprang up and through the tropical silence grew the sound of rustling foliage, unknown harmonies singing in the topmost branches. We still rowed steadily on until the river bank unexpectedly opened on the left and we glided into a broad, silent lake.

The Laguna del Saladillo. What a change of landscape! Now we were drifting between banks of almost poetic beauty. Eerie and yet fascinating jungle; where man-high grass crackled under the wind which swept round us like a hot breath from the interior of the backwoods. No trace of man. Untrodden virgin forest. Here was nature unaltered since creation, a hopeless tangle of massive rank jungle vegetation. It was a return to the saurian epoch and the appearance of a diplodocus from this nightmare scenery would have caused me no surprise.

Since it was rapidly becoming dark and a camping place had to be found quickly, we skirted the bank, looking for a suitable clearing. We had almost resigned ourselves to spending a night of discomfort in the boat, when we reached a place that seemed suited for our purpose. The first job was to clear the ground of undergrowth and find an even space for pitching the tent. In doing this we startled away a giant green lizard, a perfect inhabitant for this landscape of the tertiary age. We worked fast and before darkness had completely fallen, the tent was up and the hammocks covered with mosquito nets. We had a quick meal and then retired to sweat through a sleepless night. . . .

During the next few days I made numerous short excursions into the adjacent forest. I never ventured very far for fear of losing my way back, but I had ample opportunity of studying the forms and ways of the jungle denizens. As far as scenery was concerned the land round the Laguna del Saladillo certainly resembled the conventional "tropical paradise." Fantastically colored flowers blazed like great flaming candles against the emerald-green background of foliage. Beautiful flowering creepers hung looped from branch to branch and tree to tree in graceful festoons. These parasites were glorious in their rich and diverse variety. There was one particular kind which climbed straight up the trunk of the tree and then cascaded from the very topmost branches down to the ground at my feet in a riotous cataract of scarlet flowers. This was the most wonderful plant of all, and there drifted from its blooms a powerfully sweet smell which if breathed too long lulled the senses almost into a state of stupor. And these were only a small part of the wonders around me; more I could not see at one glance, for the depths of the forest everywhere except in the immediate vicinity lay hidden in deep twilight.

A little bush growing on the river's bank, and about a foot or so in height, attracted my attention. The bright red flowers hung in thick clusters from their stems. I stooped to pick a spray. Almost before my fingers had touched the twigs the blossoms all closed up and hung limp and lifeless in my grasp. I let them go and moved a little away. A few moments later they came to life, swinging full-blown in the sun as if they had never changed at all. This time I approached more cautiously, and stooping down, careful not to brush any part of the plant with my coat, I breathed gently over a cluster of the flowers. Again they shriveled up, and hung apparently lifeless. It was just one more of nature's amazing protective devices. Although this little bush must often have been roughly blown about by the wind, it recognized at once the soft but hostile breath of man. I looked round to investigate some less tender plant.

Not more than six feet away from me grew a fair-sized shrub hung round at about a man's height from the ground with bunches of red berries, luscious and tempting to the hungry traveler. I went nearer to see if the fruit were really edible—and turned away in sudden disgust. Instead of smooth, inviting berries they were only parasitic glutinous capsules adhering to the twigs.

Other growths which were small and green and unobtrusive made themselves especially noticeable by their penetrating and revolting smell.

One bush in particular attracted my attention. Its little branches were quite bare except for about a dozen pendent, curiously shaped leaves. Closer inspection revealed these leaves to be huge butterflies hanging indolently in the sun. They were a dying company, their splendid glittering wings now dull and shabby. I shook the bush and some of them awoke and fluttered wearily around, soon settling again on their old places to dream away their last sleep in the friendly warmth of the sun. . . .

One day I rowed myself across to the other side of the lagoon and plunged into a bamboo plantation to see what might lie beyond. I walked for some time and then realized that the plantation was considerably larger than I had thought, and that I was hopelessly lost. I pushed on in what I imagined to be the direction of the lagoon, and emerged unexpectedly into a small clearing, in the middle of which was a solitary hut. This pitiful reminder of human habitation stood primitive and wretched against the luxuriant background of the jungle. It was a picture of decaying melancholy. From the lintel of the door hung a huge gray spider's web, and as I stepped across the threshold into the dark interior a salamander flickered like green lightning between my legs and into the open. The hut was quite deserted. On the floor lay a carpet of damp leaves and in a corner were some ashes, a pair of broken tongs and a few charred bones. What awful disaster had made the owner of the hut fly in such panic-

Every day, at precisely the same hour, the heavens opened their sluices

stricken haste? I would never know. The forest, like the sea, seldom reveals its secrets.

When I came into the open again, I noticed a footpath leading into the center of a dense thicket behind the hut. I followed the narrow track and came upon a freshly filled-in grave. A stake had been driven through the middle of the mound and on it was stuck the bleached skull of a horse. All round ran a low fence of branches on which were impaled the dead and decaying bodies of hundreds of birds. The stench was intolerable. I ran from this unhallowed spot like one chased by a fiend, crashing through the undergrowth and beating the branches and twigs to either side. By good luck I emerged on the banks of the lagoon just near my boat. I had done enough exploring for that day, so I jumped in and rowed back to the camp.

Every day, at precisely the same hour, the heavens opened their sluices and drowned the world with water. Only in the tropics are such cloudbursts imaginable.

My first experience filled me with terror. From out of a clear sky came a deep rumble of thunder. There were no clouds at first but a hard gray glaze soon began spreading up from the horizon. A nervous, fearful atmosphere lay over the earth. The jungle, which a moment before was full of life, died. Birds and beasts crouched down in their safe hiding places. Now a parrot wishing to shatter the lonely silence would scream out from beneath his leafy screen. Soon terror overcame even his longing for companionship, and he too was silent. The gray above turned to a deep midnight blue and tatters of black clouds hung down from the sky like ragged veils. Once again nature seemed to take a deep breath and wait. Then the heavens broke, and fell to earth in a solid sheet of water. From every branch and bough ceaseless waterfalls poured to the ground, churning the dry dust into a black swamp of mud.

Then it was over. As quickly as it had come the storm was gone, and the sun shone down with renewed energy. Nature awoke to new life. Myriads of insects swarmed out of the rotting timber of dead tree trunks and danced in the sun, swirling like evanescent puffs of smoke. Hundreds of glittering hummingbirds shot through the air like little arrows, each species uttering its own distinctive "hum-m-m." They flitted about like living prismatic jewels, changing their burnished colors with every movement, as their plumage reflected the sun in a brilliance of gold-green or crimson lake. They paused and hovered before the giant flowers, creating quite a noticeable breeze with their tiny wings. When one had selected a flower for himself he drove at it like a bullet and rammed his beak deep down into the velvet cavity. There he remained for a few moments, head hidden in the flower while he ate the insects and honey, wings humming outside to keep his tiny body horizontal. When he emerged, his head would be covered with pollen which he deposited in the next flower he visited. And so nature uses these birds, little bigger than bumble-bees, to fertilize the great jungle flowers.

At sunset the flamboyant colors of the forest died. Everything assumed a gray monotony. A chill hung on the air, welcome and dangerous to the hot, sweating body. One listened to the intense silence of night with nervous alarm. The imagination worked strongly. Things appeared that were not really there; lianas turned to snakes, cacti resembled scorpions; fireflies danced like will-o'-the-wisps, and bats were vampires and dragons.

The fear passed. Slowly the eye became accustomed to the

This reservoir of tropical nature seemed to be monstrous and inexhaustible

darkness, and slowly the ear, hardened by the ceaseless roar of a big city, became aware of the little sounds which quivered out of the night.

I shall never forget the evening when I went rowing alone on the lagoon. I pulled the boat out through the black water streaked with weeds and swaying plants. In the distance echoed the song of my natives as they sat round the fire, drying their sweat-soaked clothes. The vast evening concert of the forest had just begun. Millions of frogs made the night horrible with their harsh noise, accompanied by the strident trilling of legions of crickets and grasshoppers. A deep sustained bass note served to balance this jungle cacophony.

I pulled in the oars and sat motionless in the drifting boat as I tried to realize the incredible luxuriance of the wild life around me. This reservoir of tropical nature seemed to me to be monstrous and inexhaustible. The forest lives unceasingly and never dies. A tree falls, and three new shoots spring out of the old trunk, nourishing themselves on their decaying parent. Cut a clearing in the miasmal swamps and in less than two weeks it has all closed in again with thicker, ranker growth than ever before. One animal dies and millions of insects thrive on the rotting corpse.

The jungle lives and multiplies. From day to day, from night to night, since the gray dawn of creation, there has been war, the bitter, merciless war between life and death. The weak succumb; none but the strongest survive to die a natural death. The only law the jungle recognizes is the great cycle of life and death, death supporting life. Decaying trees give birth to fresh green shoots of ferns; the ferns nourish the lesser animals who in turn fall prey to the carnivora, and these in death make food and breeding-places for all the millions of insects. And so it goes on throughout creation. Out of death comes life—life in abundance. . . .

I learned one useful tip from my black servants—the art of resting in the wilds. The natives need no chairs to sit on, whether in the jungle or out of it, for they relax by squatting down on their haunches in their own peculiar way with the weight of the body resting on the knees. As soon as one has grown accustomed to this peculiar attitude and the muscles have acquired the necessary resilience it becomes a pleasant position of rest in the comfortless jungle, and it has the added advantage of being practicable in places where boggy ground or sharp stones make sitting impossible. There is also less likelihood of one's body becoming infested by swarms of red ants or other stinging and creeping insects. Besides, should any sudden danger arise, it is easier to spring up from a squatting than from a sitting position.

There are two ways of squatting. One can either rest with the whole flat of the foot on the ground and the knees under the armpits, or with all the weight of the body carried on the balls of the feet and the elbows resting on the knees. If one occasionally changes from the one position to the other, the muscles will never get tired. After a little practice I became so adept at balancing that I could even read and write while squatting. . . .

I stayed a week in this wild paradise, and then decided to send the boat together with half the crew up the river towards Dajabon, the frontier post, while I myself would take the remaining three blacks and strike southwards through the jungle, hoping to meet the boat in the neighborhood of Dajabon.

I unloaded some provisions and then watched the *Brush-by* disappear up the Massacre River. After we had waved it round the last bend we struck tent and packed up. The negroes hoisted the heavy bundles onto their backs and secured them with a thong of leather passing round their foreheads after the fashion of South American Indians. Then we set out in single file.

My jungle "safari" had begun.

IV. JUNGLE MAGIC

FOR the rest of my life I shall be haunted by the memory of that cross-country journey.

According to my extremely inaccurate map the distance from Laguna del Saladillo to Dajabon was no more than a day's traveling. The reality taught me, amongst other things, an unbounded respect for the fertile imagination of the cartographer, who had even gone so far as to spot the course of the Massacre River with highsounding names and towns, marked at least as large as London or New York. It was too late to recall the boat so I struggled forwards, hung round like a Christmas tree with rucksack, revolver, cartridges, binoculars, and a machete; scrambling through the all but impenetrable jungle in a temperature of 130 degrees; every moment getting caught up like Absalom in the ubiquitous branches and having to call back the natives to release me from my undignified captivity. Often palms and giant ferns closed in the trail to the proverbial needle's eye, and then we had to crawl on our stomachs.

There was always a steady drip from the leaves above, soaking into soil that had been sodden since the beginning of time. Orange, purple, and scarlet fungi sprouted from the rotting mould. Once we disturbed an army of tiny red ants who immediately swarmed up the bare legs of my natives. With one concerted yell they sprang into the air and vanished into the gloom of the surrounding forest. I spent many long hours of calling and searching in the green twilight of the woods before I had them all assembled again.

A little farther on, when I was leading, a huge dead tree trunk leant across our path. By stooping we could have passed under it, but I pushed at it impatiently and something fell heavily on my head, jamming my topee over my eyes. I had broken the great tree clean off. Luckily for me the three-foot log that struck my head was no more than a mass of dust and splinters. I jumped backwards, partly because I was not quite sure what had happened, but also because I thought a box of lighted matches had fallen down my back. I could not locate the "flame" for it seemed to burn in ten, twenty, different places at the same time. Actually, a party of fire-ants had fallen from the tree and dropped down my neck, so there was nothing for it but to strip naked and let the three negroes pick the infuriated ants off my body one by one.

Many times on our march I was reduced to a state of impotent rage and distraction by the plaguing insects. All day long the blow-flies tormented us and at night the mosquitoes carried on the attack. The latter approached so silently that their bite was the first warning of their presence. To avoid becoming a victim of malaria, I dosed myself with a daily ration of quinine; indeed without this valuable prophylactic a long stay in the jungle would be impossible for any white man.

Even vegetable enemies were not lacking. There were hook-shaped, thorny shoots, which hung down from high branches and twined round the neck of the unsuspecting traveler like a green hangman's noose. Any attempt to drag them quickly off left long, deep scratches on the face and neck. More dangerous than these was a strange species of palm tree whose trunk was covered with red clusters of tiny thorns. If one brushed too close to this tree the poisonous barbs dug into the bare skin and set up acute irritation and feverishness.

All through the heavy silence of the night I could hear the scratching and scraping of the industrious ants. I imitated them as far as the scratching was concerned, for I had no peace from insects during the darkness although I took every possible precaution. In the evening the mosquito netting over my hammock was always covered with grotesquely winged moths, mantis, beetles, and mosquitoes which I proceeded to brush off before retiring. I then slipped adroitly under the net and cleared the blankets of cockroaches. This done, I climbed into the hammock, and lying on my back I searched the inside of the net for stray mosquitoes which I tracked down with the aid of my electric torch. Although I killed all I could see, I always woke up the next morning to find many others clinging to the netting, gorged and bloated with my blood.

Out in the forest there was never any question of sleeping soundly through the night and waking at dawn cool and refreshed. At the best one only dozed intermittently, sweating in a damp oven heat. More often than not one lay wide-eyed the whole night through, gazing at the tangle of branches and little patches of starlit sky above.

The night seemed endless. Just before dawn a hush fell over the forest and a thin gray film of light spread across the sky. Another pause, while the sun pushed a narrow beam over the horizon and a pale ray of yellow light would pierce the mysterious darkness of the undergrowth, scattering the gloom in its path.

Each object as the sunbeam struck it shone with a glorious radiance. A lilac orchid opened slowly into exotic bloom under the benign warmth of the sun. A thousand glittering threads woven into an intricate pattern stretched across a near-by bush. The spider lurked in the shadows watching; awaiting the moment when chance should deliver into his silver net some tasty victim for breakfast. On a sloping tree trunk a pair of iguanas, survivors from the antediluvian era, met in the sunlight and played their little drama of love. A yellow-breasted parrot cleft the shaft of light and vanished again into the darkness.

Two toucans, ridiculous birds with their unwieldy-looking beaks, settled on a branch and peered at me questioningly as if to say, "You are no part of *our* world." Their plumage glistened in a jazz symphony of garish colors and even their beaks shaped like swollen bananas were striped in brilliant hues. They cocked their heads first on one side and then on the other as they gazed at me. At last, having evidently decided that I was a harmless creature, they started the day's work. With their apparently cumbersome beaks the two companions performed an astonishing variety of duties. First they combed and preened their feathers. When their toilet was completed they pecked playfully at the berries around them. Then they plucked them off the bush and gave a juggling performance by tossing each berry up in the air, catching it in their beaks when it came down, swallowing the fruit, and spitting the stones at me below. When the light moved away from them, the two birds composed themselves for sleep, heads drawn in, beaks tucked under their feathers as far as they would go, and tails sticking vertically up in the air.

The ground beneath me, which now received the heat of the sun, was riddled with small holes from whence there presently emerged little land-crabs who basked in the warmth and waved their claws frantically about in the air like stock-brokers during a boom.

By this time I was exceedingly hungry. I aroused my snoring natives who soon had a delicious breakfast simmering over the campfire. After the morning meal I went exploring in the forest or, when opportunity offered, I set up my easel to do a bit of painting. My pictures progressed with difficulty for I had no sooner arranged the tripod firmly on the boggy ground than the whole canvas was covered with inch-long ants. I managed to stave off the bulk of this invasion by smearing a ring of white lead round each of the legs of the easel, but even then several of the most persistent ants, not to be held off, ate their way through the encircling paint, and climbed successfully aloft.

When I finally got to work, my black attendants generally stood round about me and studied my labors with admiring

Two toucans . . . settled on a branch and peered at me

eyes. On one occasion I found a tube of sardine paste in my paint-box, placed there by Bonaparte, my faithful cook, who thought it contained paint. I squeezed out a few inches on to my palette and continued painting for some minutes. Then I opened my knapsack, cut a large slice of bread, and looked critically at the paint-streaked palette. Three pairs of astounded negro eyes followed my every action. I wavered —or so it seemed to them—between cinnabar-red and sardine-brown. Finally I decided for the brown and spread it thickly on the bread with my palette knife. Their eyes almost dropped out of their heads as I devoured the bread with evident enjoyment!

I eventually explained the joke to Bonaparte who laughed uproariously at it. He was the best camp cook I have ever come across, for he could produce a good meal in face of almost insuperable difficulties. The reason for this was that he used nothing but wild fruit and vegetables, which he served up in countless different ways. His chef d'œuvre, a soup brewed from palm shoots, was really delicious. There was only one dish of his to which I could not accustom myself and I left the relish of that to my black servants. It was toasted ants!

In spite of "Bon's" efforts a vegetarian diet for days on end became extremely monotonous, so I varied it whenever I could by picking off with my revolver the largest birds we came across during the day's march. Of these the toucans were far the most palatable. To avoid any risk of catching dysentery, drinking water always had to be boiled and vegetables washed in permanganate of potash, which added greatly to the trouble of preparing a meal. Nevertheless "Bon" was always good-tempered and willing. I was lucky to have found such a good fellow for my expedition.

Hitherto we had been traveling at an easy pace, but now, owing to the moist, unhealthy atmosphere of the forest, I determined to push on with greater speed. This was easier to decide on than to do. Whichever way we turned, we were faced with an impenetrable wall of jungle. At first it seemed as if we had reached the end of the forest, but closer inspection revealed the barrier as a strong curtain of branches woven together by innumerable slender lianas. Backwards and forwards I ran like an animal behind the bars of a cage. In vain—nowhere could I find the smallest gap; everywhere rose the wall before me, of equal thickness, equally impenetrable. It was hopeless. In desperation I grasped at the branches and shook them violently. A stabbing pain ran up my arms and as I snatched my hands away I saw that they were bathed in blood. The jungle had shown its teeth!

After five weary hours we succeeded in hacking our way out. This had to be done with the greatest care for one never knew where a snake was lurking or which decaying tree was the home of ants who would swarm over us in vicious, stinging hordes at the slightest provocation. A hundred yards beyond hung another barrier stronger than the first. For nine long days we chopped our way inch by inch through the wilderness, sometimes in such darkness that my negroes were indistinguishable at a distance of five yards.

Today it was even darker although the forest was more open than of late. When we reached a small clearing I glanced up at the sky and I was horrified to see, instead of the usual cerulean blue, a limitless expanse of dull gray vapors that were slowly and heavily descending upon us. In a short space the heavens assumed a uniform inky blackness. The sun was quite invisible. Something frightful was about to happen. The young negroes looked anxiously

When opportunity offered, I set up my easel

towards me, hoping that I at least could explain this strange behavior of nature. I was as ignorant as they, but I assumed that we were in for a thunderstorm. And what a thunderstorm! It was a terrestrial cataclysm of incredible dimensions.

With feverish haste I pitched tent in a sheltered spot, making the guy-ropes doubly sure with heavy logs and lashing the tent-poles securely to the nearest trees. We had scarcely finished when a flash of jagged lightning flickered across the black sky, illuminating the forest in a sulphurous glow. After a breathless pause came a long, distant rumble of thunder that shook the ground beneath us. It was as if Nature incarnate had fallen to earth and was shattering the world with her pounding heart.

Then a deluge of great, ice-cold drops rattled down from above. Soon the surrounding ground was a morass. Streams of water came pouring into the tent and the four of us had to huddle close together in order to enjoy some slight measure of warmth and dryness.

The rain was now augmented by great gusts of wind, and a storm of gargantuan violence swept over the tops of the trees. We below suffered only a small part of this fury owing to the sheltering forest but what we did get was more than enough. Tremendous detonations like salvoes from a hundred guns shook the world around us. The cloudburst assumed the proportions of a vast waterfall, hiding the whole forest from our sight. I thought in a moment of panic that the weight of water would crush the little tent flat upon us.

The rain was decreasing but worse was to follow. Immense electrical discharges now took place. Blue flames blazed up from the ground. A blinding ribbon of light from east to west tore the inky firmament in two. Three times that fearful flash shot across the sky, revealing the lianas stretched up like giant spiders' webs against the flaming heavens.

It was a moment of inhuman terror.

The frightened natives crouched close to each other and to me with little whimpering cries of fear.

The hurricane (for I afterwards learnt that it was the same one which swept its path of destruction across Florida and the Antilles, leaving half San Domingo City in ruins) shrieked above us with tripled fury. Through a tear in the tent canvas I could see the luminous forest outside. The lianas that a moment before had hung in giant webs from their parent trees now streamed aloft like the newly combed tresses of some titanic gorgon. Bushes flew through the air; mighty branches were hurled about like straws.

I received a heavy blow on the head followed by an aching pain. Something warm trickled down my forehead and over my eyes. I wiped it away with my hand. It was only sweat!

Then in a flash—as it came—the storm was gone. A continuous patter of water still rained from above, but this came only from the dripping foliage. The sky was clear and a blazing sun shone down as though nothing untoward had happened, bathing the forest in its grateful warmth.

The havoc around us was terrific.

Broken branches lay scattered about in fearful confusion, while the lesser vegetation in all its manifold forms was crushed and pounded to a pulp as if it had been thrown into an enormous cement-mixer.

High above sounded the clear trill of a bell-bird.

The jungle soon forgets.

A cavalcade of little dove-like birds came hopping gayly down the path, looking for all the world like a battalion of street-sweepers as they cleared the path of worms. They approached us across the clearing without the slightest sign of fear, marched by, and disappeared into the darkness of the woods on the other side.

Our soaking clothes and belongings soon dried in the still warm air; and, when we had eaten a meal, we broke camp and pushed forward in an attempt to reach human habitations as quickly as possible. Thanks to the storm our progress now was even slower than before. At every step one sank ankle-deep into the soft, viscous slime from which oozed bubbles of some foul-smelling liquid; and before the next step could be taken the hinder foot had to be pulled out with a loud "plop!" It was like walking through a river of treacle. The air was permeated with the sickly odor of rankness and decay as a result of evaporation from the rotting vegetation.

The heavy rain had brought out a new peril to hinder our advance. In passing through the jungle one had to be wary not to brush against any overhanging foliage, for, silently and painlessly, the blood-sucking leeches would drop from above and attach themselves to any unprotected portion of the body. These disgusting worms were all the more insidious in that they gave no warning of their presence by inflicting any sensation or pain. The only way of discovering them was either to get one of the natives to look carefully for them or to wipe one's neck and forehead and thereby brush the bloated creatures off. These leeches cannot inflict any direct injury, but a large loss of blood weakens the body and renders it far more susceptible than usual to fever and other jungle diseases. Consequently I was more afraid of these clammy animals than almost any other danger that threatened, and, as it turned out, I was justified in my fear.

Under such conditions of discomfort as these, the carping question will often arise: what is the *use* of such an undertaking? How much pleasanter and probably just as interesting it would be to sit at home in an easy chair with a roof overhead, far from all storms and from the uncharted, ever-threatening jungle, and to read about it all; to enjoy the thrills without the risks! But, in spite of all these arguments, there are wonderful sensations and glorious experiences that the armchair-lazer and city-dweller cannot even dream of. They have never felt the irresistible call that draws a man into the wilds. Nor can they realize that a great reward is offered (and gained by so few fortunate mortals), the sight of some corner of the earth which human eyes have never seen before.

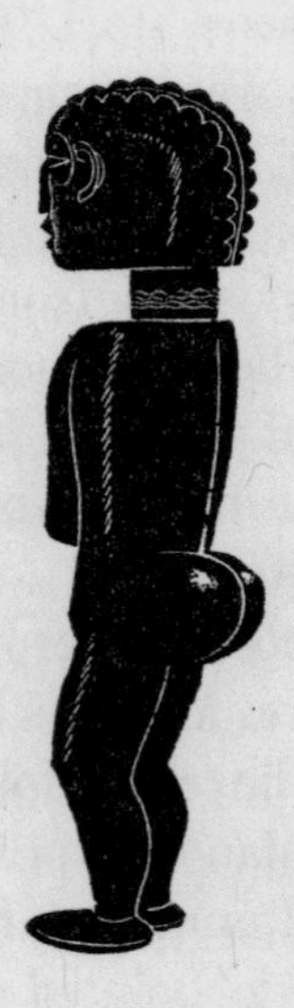

The next day we reached Dajabon.

Here too the storm had raged. Giant trees of the forest were laid low; negro huts were overturned and scattered; the whole village was in hopeless confusion. The *Brush-by* had arrived safely several days before, but now as a result of the storm it was leaking badly and half full of water. My poor Rauri lay in a hut, racked with fever.

"Malaria," said the black village doctor. "It will soon be gone. The crisis is already over."

Under normal conditions the river was only navigable as far as Dajabon, but after the torrential downpour of the day before it was brimming over its banks and consequently open for a considerable distance further upstream.

I was determined not to give up my fixed project to reach the Cordillera del Monte Christo and this opportunity of traveling onwards by water seemed too good to be missed. Since the river would soon start falling, we had to get to work quickly. The boat was dragged out on to the bank by the concerted efforts of myself and the five boys, and we soon caulked the holes and had her seaworthy again. I bought some more provisions from the village shop and stowed them aboard. The next morning we started off, all except Ford whom I had left with instructions to look after the sick Rauri and take him down to Fort Liberté at the first opportunity that offered.

So we set off again shortly after dawn, rowing briskly up the swiftly flowing stream. As far as La Palba, the last village on Haitian territory, the river followed a fairly straight course, then it curved inland towards Santo Domingo.

On our way we passed numerous floating islands and trees which showed, as Ottavio pointed out, that the river was still rising. The banks were flooded to a considerable depth. Trees and large bushes grew out of the water, their long, low branches stretching across the surface of the river as if to bar our way.

I sat, as I generally did, in the stern of the boat, attending to the intricate business of steering. Now and again the wind swept masses of dead foliage from the forest into the river. A dying orchid fell from above, landed on my head, and slipped into the muddy water which meandered slowly and lazily from the mountains to the distant sea.

My idle glance was suddenly arrested by a break in the dull continuity of the scenery. A long stone wall rising out of the water—what building had the hand of man raised in the midst of this desolation? Perhaps the ruins of a rampart built by the old conquistador Granados? Visions of the past rose before my eyes. . . .

Words of command rang out.

Bearded adventurers in heavy armor disembarking from the great galleon anchored down the bay. Pikes and swords clanking; cannons gaping at the silent forest with their hungry mouths.

Over all, alarm and confusion.

The old-fashioned, pot-bellied sailing ship had run aground on a sandbank, immovable. It might be days or even weeks before the galleon could float again and return to the open sea.

But inland, somewhere behind the mysterious jungle, lay the fabulous mountain of gold.

That *must* be found.

The day before, a party of Spaniards hunting for food in the jungle had captured two trembling Indians. These natives had never left their native jungle nor ever been near the mountains, but the Spaniards could not know that.

"*Caramba*, you dogs, do you still refuse the secret of your golden treasure?"

The whips hissed through the air and cracked once more against the bleeding backs of the captives. Of course the Indians could not understand the questions, nor could the Spaniards understand their replies, if any had been given; but the Indians were silent. They must be *made* to understand, and the universal language that the Spaniards spoke with such fluency was brought into use. Cruelty—the Inquisition was a past master of the art, and whips were the kindest instruments of torture. Yet when a few days later two mangled bodies were thrown into the river, the Spaniards were no wiser than before.

Another expedition brought back three more captives. They were more intelligent—and more amenable. Screaming under the most hellish pains that the twisted mentality of man could invent, a quivering native pointed upstream. He also died but he had served his purpose. A fair-sized party led by Granados struck inland towards the mountains in search of Eldorado. They were never seen again, but before the night was out the others knew their fate.

Darkness closed down on the half-deserted ship. Even the men on board were nervous, fearing silent night. The only sound was the swishing of the river as it rippled against the bows of the ship. The green wall of jungle still held its secret terrors, thin wisps of fever mist crept aboard through every crack and cranny; the men whispered together in frightened undertones. . . .

Suddenly the silence broke.

There were no yells. Just the twanging of bow-strings and the hiss of burning arrows as they swept across the deck. The outcries of the Spaniards died still-born: the croaking throats were choked with blood.

In the long silence that followed, the swishing of the river could be clearly heard as it rippled round the ship and its dead crew.

A massacre! Massacre River: hence its name?

Was the overgrown stone wall the last witness of that tragic expedition? Four hundred years have drawn across the scene an impenetrable veil. The river still ripples to the sea—today as yesterday, tomorrow as today.

The white man in the jungle lives and dies a conqueror, or if not a conqueror, always a fighter.

The native is a part of the jungle just as much as the great trees and creepers. He carries in him the silence and the mystery, the secrets and the darkness of the forest. He is its servant, understands its moods, and regards himself as part of its creation.

It almost seems that should a native stay motionless for long, he would strike roots into the ground, and grow upwards. Lianas would hang down from his shoulders—spiders run over his feet, lizards climb up his body, and parrots nest in his hair. The native never aspires to be a conqueror like the white man; he surrenders himself unconditionally to the omnipotence of his surroundings.

The farther we progressed, the wilder and more desolate became the country. It was extraordinary and terrifying how the loneliness weighed upon me; almost frantically I searched the banks for signs of human habitation. I tried in vain to persuade myself that no sane people would settle in this region of desolation, far from their kind and cut off from the rest of the world. There never *was* anybody, but I always hoped.

Hour after hour resounded the monotonous creaking of the oars against the pins as the four black bodies swayed rhythmically backwards and forwards. The native art of rowing appeared to consist chiefly in throwing the maximum amount of water into the air with the blades of oars. Yet in spite of all the wasted energy we advanced fairly rapidly.

The sun sank below the tree tops leaving only a pale red glow in the sky. The boys were getting tired and rowing jerkily, and even I dozed as I steered. Unexpectedly a heavy shower of rain fell, filling the boat ankle-deep with water. I sat hunched in the stern, miserably aware that whereas I was drenched through, my natives were quite dry, the rain having run straight off their oily naked backs.

We started bailing out the boat and I saw to my horror that the bottom was leaking again. Water was pouring in as fast as we emptied it out. It looked as though our expedition was going to have a fatal ending for if the boat went down we should have to swim for it and the river was infested with carnivorous creatures. Even if we escaped them we should have the unpleasant alternative of swimming about till we drowned, for the flooded, overgrown banks offered no landing place to a weary swimmer.

Without perceptible change the tropical night spread over the sky. There were glittering stars above, but no moon, and in the dark the danger of catastrophe was doubled. A moment before we were faced with the prospect of sinking slowly but surely in our sieve-like boat, now there was the added risk of capsizing in the darkness. Two of us bailed and the other three rowed cautiously. Now and again the bottom of the boat scraped over some hard object, probably a submerged tree stump or rock.

The overhanging branches buffeted our heads unmercifully.

It seemed as if we had been struggling for hours. I lit the boat's lamp, more for comfort than for utility; its light scarcely pierced the gloom for more than a yard or two.

A large clod of grass-grown earth swirled by. Perched on top was a coiled-up snake philosophically awaiting its doom. Shadowy night birds swept like phantoms across the surface of the river. Here and there some creature emerged from the black waters, snapped at an invisible prey, and sank out of sight again.

We could only push on with the greatest difficulty and effort. Inside the boat new leaks had developed and the water was rising visibly in spite of our frantic exertions. The damp night air chilled us. For hours on end my feet had been soaking in the icy water at the bottom of the boat.

Wearily I suppressed a fit of shivering.

I wondered whether it would not be best to run the boat ashore at the next possible break in the jungle and spend the night sitting in a tree. It would be a more than doubtful experiment considering the conditions. A pitch-dark night, an unknown forest, and not the slightest chance of any boat passing up or down the river for several days. On the whole it would be better to row on. Our boat would scarcely move it was so waterlogged, but we progressed slowly in a last hopeless effort.

Suddenly a few tiny pinpricks of light flickered out from the opposite bank.

Men in the middle of the jungle! A new energy filled our

bodies as we bucketed the now almost completely submerged boat towards the guiding light.

I held the lantern out towards the bank. There, not six yards away, was a crumbling landing stage. I tied the boat up and stumbled ashore.

V. TROPICAL FEVER

I HAD not realized how completely exhausted I was until I scrambled on to the landing place and fell on my knees. My legs were almost too weak to support me. However, with the assistance of the natives, who had done much more work than I and yet were not half so weary, I walked towards the welcoming light.

The settlement was tiny. It had only two streets, and the whole place was pervaded by a dank, earthy smell. Primitive mud-plastered huts and wooden shacks alternated with one another, while some of the more elementary dwellings were built of tree bark or bamboo. All were in the last stages of collapse: many of them tilting over to one side after the manner, but with none of the grace, of the leaning tower of

Pisa. The luxuriant vegetation grew high around and in between, half hiding the houses, if such they could be called, from view. The only sign of life and friendliness was a rusty, crooked street lamp, whose already feeble flame was reduced to less than half by the thick cloud of mosquitoes buzzing round it. It was a nightmare scene, verging on the imaginings of a madman. The flickering yellow light illuminated crazy huts in every stage of decay framed in velvet pall of densest black.

The forest breathed out waves of moist air.

My head was throbbing wildly. I thought for one awful moment this might be a feverish illusion. And then I saw dark-skinned natives clustering round me.

With one accord the village woke from sleep and the hoarse, angry barking of a hundred mongrels shattered the heavy silence. Round, questioning eyes gazed at us in mild astonishment. An ebony-colored child drew himself erect with the help of my gaiter and wiped his nose abstractedly on my knee. The grown-ups remained shyly in the background.

Undecided as to what the next step should be I waited a minute and considered how I could best introduce myself to this kindly, timid folk. Then out of the shadowy throng of whispering natives came a lighter-colored, fair-haired man who advanced towards me.

"I have been expecting you." This strange greeting which fitted in so well with the rest of that unearthly scene came in perfect English, spoken with a curiously colorless intonation.

"You are the artist. For the last few weeks, on the river and in the jungle, you have been closely watched."

A white duck suit, now creased and far from clean, hung on the shoulders of the emaciated skeleton as from a clothes hanger. This bony man was just another figure in the nightmare with his expressionless eyes blazing out of a fever-shrunken head. Bushy black eyebrows contrasted strangely with the straggling gray mustache that hung down over his mouth and chin. He could not be human. I knew I was suffering from some ghastly delusion, that I must turn and run away. But as always happens in a nightmare my legs refused to move.

I checked my thoughts. Better not think at all than think like this. Obviously the man before me was alive. I knew that as soon as he gripped my wrist with his fleshless fingers. He said, "You'll come with me?" and I said nothing, partly because there was nothing to say, but chiefly because I was too tired to say anything. So I made no answer, but turned and followed the man. More to himself than to me, he growled:

"Damned glad to see a white man in this God-blasted fever hole. Doesn't often happen. I'll introduce myself; my name was once Hickman—that was a long time ago."

He was silent as if pondering the memories conjured up by the utterance of his name. Then we entered a house which seemed a little less derelict than the rest of the negro huts around. It was simply built, consisting of one large room that did duty as parlor, dining room, bedroom, and kitchen, all at the same time. A wobbly, rough-sawn table stood in the middle of the room. Above it hung a mosquito-encircled lamp. My strength was returning; it had been mostly numbness that had rendered me so helpless. I studied the scene more closely. There was a plank-bed in one corner with some brown blankets lying untidily on it, just as he had thrown them when he got up to fetch me. I knew afterwards that it was not his bed at all for he invariably slept in a hammock. The plank-bed was reserved for me. On the shelves against the wall were a few rows of books looking curiously lonely and out of place in their jungle surroundings.

At that moment my attention was distracted by Hickman who was opening a squat round bottle. He called for a boy to bring some glasses. There was still something uncanny about this man that I could not understand. Perhaps the books against the wall would tell me something about his past, his education, and his interests, and so give me some clue as to his strangeness. I walked over to the shelves but he was so intent on the bottle that he took no notice. There were four rows of books piled together pell-mell, most of them dealing with the history of the West Indies, but there were also some volumes on botany and toxicology, and a few philosophical treatises by English, German, and French authors.

Hickman was now watching me intently, a cat-and-mouse look, but he said nothing until I had finished my inspection of his treasures. Then, when I addressed him, he replied in clumsy, ill-pronounced, but quite understandable German. He removed his eyes from me to the bottle of spirits and uttered his sentences so slowly and deliberately that it sounded as though he were speaking to himself.

"My father," he began, "was one of the political refugees from Germany in 1848. After he had left the Fatherland for ever, he settled at first in Galveston, Texas. He stayed there for a few years and then moved on; he had the *Wanderlust* to see tropical countries and, above all, the West Indies. In Port-au-Prince, which he finally chose as his home, he secured an influential position as adviser-in-chief to the then President of the Republic, Sylvai Salnave, and in accordance with his status married the daughter of the English ambassador.

"Shortly after my birth my father and the President lost their lives during a revolutionary riot. I was therefore brought up by my mother who always spoke English with me, but at the age of seven I went to a Catholic seminary at Port-au-Prince where I received a good general education from a priest who spoke nothing but German. Later in life I learned the Creole dialect from the natives amongst whom I lived.

"When I was eighteen my mother sent me to the United States to take a technical course at one of the Northern universities. I was very unwilling to go but my mother was so anxious for me to have some means of livelihood that I agreed. When I got there I was nearly frozen to death in that bitter climate. I hated the country and I hated the people and most of all I hated the civilization. Civilization makes mental eunuchs of men. Under its influences their intellects become sterile and they lose all interest in life except for filling their distended stomachs and sleeping in warm corners. I held out for three years, hiding my misery and hatred, and then I returned rejoicing like a child back to my tropical home. Since then, for thirty-odd years, I have never left Haiti; I have only one connection with the world beyond—my books.

"Here in the forest is my home. The love of the forest is rooted in me, never more to be escaped or thrown off. I was born with a longing for loneliness."

Hickman ended his rather sketchy and stilted narrative with a long draught of tafia. Then he slowly combed his straggling beard with his fingers. His hand dropped down to his lap and he sat motionless as stone. A long pause followed. I held my breath and great cold beads of sweat dropped from my forehead. The silence was terrifying. My gaze traveled across to the doorway. A cat crept into view, trod on a scorpion, and—as though struck by lightning—tumbled over. Hickman noticed nothing; he was too deeply busied with his own thoughts.

Suddenly his head jerked up and his fathomless eyes stared into mine. "And so you see," he went on as if there had been no gap in the story, "after a time a white man becomes a part of the jungle. It happens to everyone who chooses to live in the forest; there is no escape. A man will always come back to the only place where peace and happiness are to be found. Only in this wonderful solitude can the soul live.

Only here comes the perfect realization that civilization is nothing, that a civilized man is a nonentity; for in the forest the man who fancies himself the lord of the world crumples up with impotence before an omnipotent Nature. . . ."

He laughed. It sounded like the bleating of an elderly goat.

"Once upon a time, long ago—very long ago—I met a white Haitian in the United States while I was studying there. For the first time in twenty-five years he had returned to the so-called civilized world. The experiment was a failure. Away from the jungle he was lost; everything had become strange and unfamiliar. It was a terrible example of the ruin that civilization can bring. Half the night long he sat up in his bed, stroking the cool, clean sheets and mumbling to himself and laughing. He bought tobacco by the pound because he liked the large parcel it made; in the jungle a handful of tobacco had lasted him for weeks. The new life amongst civilization completely dazzled him. He lost all standards of sense and proportion and delighted in indulging his craziest fancies. Every morning he went to the barber and had his gnarled, calloused hands manicured by a girl there; then he went out and grabbled in the first dirty puddle he came across, splashing about like any street urchin and laughing at the stupidity of our effeminate civilization.

"One morning he quietly vanished. Years later, long after I had returned to my solitary life, we met again. This time it was on our beloved island, far inland, far from other white men. How we laughed and shook our heads over that strange distant world where men were no longer men but puppets of glass."

Hickman moistened his throat with another gulp of rum. His vacant gaze wandered about the room and finally settled on the bookcase.

"All the same, one never forgets," he continued in a more sentimental strain. "Not for the wealth of empires would a man sell his memories of the past. Especially in this forgotten hole, where they're the only things of any value a man possesses. I have seen planters, jaundiced with fever, and prospectors, hardbitten as granite, sob like little children when a scratching gramophone record has started to quaver out some well-remembered song. . . .

"Slowly, unbelievably slowly, comes the change; the transmutation from civilized man to backwoodsman. A white man comes into the jungle. At first everything is strange and curious to him—then comes the terrible realization that all he has learnt, all the knowledge he has gathered in the outer world, is nothing, is absolutely meaningless and void.

"Cut off from civilization, he finds himself surrounded by a thousand unknown dangers. He looks wildly round for support—and finds none. The surging crowd of streets and tenements is gone and he must fight against the overwhelming solitude alone. When a man has survived those first three solitary months, he begins to notice the changing of his inmost self. The thinly spread veneer of civilization cracks. He can feel his soul growing and a new rhythm of life being born within him. He becomes introspective, and is faced with age-old problems he has never known before. His thoughts are lost in confusion, wondering that the inner life and experience should make him sentimental, while the outer circumstances deny all sentiment. He is often possessed of an involuntary rigid brutality; he becomes an iron-willed maniac, accepting the challenge of Nature, determined to fight her and to conquer.

"But inevitably, in the long course of years the jungle wins and, like a deceitful woman, it lures the white man, drawing him slowly and imperceptibly into its clinging embrace. It absorbs him and transforms him. And there is no end to the transformation, for there is always the building up of a new soul and a new understanding. There is really no end. . . .

"Of course I'm not referring to the whites who live and work in an office in Port-au-Prince or Cap Haitien. Those men have every comfort and, because they are always carefully shielded from the baneful influence of the jungle, they are never in danger of losing their shallow civilization.

"No—I am speaking only of the man who goes into the jungle alone and in whose clear, cool eyes the lust for adventure burns; the man who can understand the language of the forest, who has the spirit of freedom. *He* is the man whom all the world should hear and respect."

The old man paused in his tirade and wiped his forehead in agitation. Suddenly he slapped his hand on his neck, squeezed something between his forefinger and thumb and held out a squashed brown mosquito towards me.

"Have you ever heard of the *anopheles*, the yellow-fever carrier? Here's one for you!"

He threw the insect on the floor and spat on it, rubbing the spittle into the ground with his foot. A gust of wind drove moist air through the rustling bamboo walls.

A burning sensation of feverishness swept over me, and I shook with an uncontrollable terror which only passed when Hickman's strange, dry voice resumed its discourse.

"It isn't the savage animals that frighten the white man." Every word rang hard and sharp against the whispering background of trees. "Wild beasts give warning of their attack. One can see them and hear them, and be on guard. No! They are not the real danger. The invisible world is the real danger; the creatures that cannot be fought. There are the malaria mosquitoes and the clouds of poisonous insects, always waiting to catch a man who is off his guard: there is the insidious fer-de-lance, instant death lurking near the incautious foot, and gigantic electric storms such as only the tropics know. All these are the real perils that beset a man in the jungle. They are the true enemies of man.

"Treacherous rapids and unsuspected whirlpools threaten his boat. Death and annihilation dog his footsteps everywhere. The jungle is as silent as the thousand-headed death it shields and this silence clutches at the soul. With every thump of the heart, every beat of the pulse, terror whips the mind to wakefulness. Destruction awaits the man who for one fleeting instant forgets his solitary weapon against death, and that weapon is—*unremitting caution.* A single failure—today, tomorrow, or in years—means death.

"In this eternal silence, in this unceasing effort of waking and watching, even the strongest nerves will crack at last.

"A day or two ago I went down to the river. It was evening and nearly dark, so I felt my way along the railing that led to the landing stage. A sudden warning flashed through my brain. *Never do that.* I snatched back my hand and put it in my pocket, realizing as soon as I had done it how foolishly nervous I had been. I laughed at myself and then, out of curiosity, walked back the way I had come, examining the rail. Scarcely a foot from where I had lifted my hand sat a tiny green lizard whose bite according to tradition meant almost instantaneous death. It was forest instinct that made me draw back my hand in the nick of time and thereby save my life.

"Another time I was standing on the edge of the jungle

and I absent-mindedly shook a hanging liana. *Plomp*—something fell on to my shoulder, glided over my hand to the ground, and vanished without biting me. It was one of the most deadly snakes known to man and no more in length than a lead pencil. Since then I've always looked carefully before I catch hold of anything.

"Some time after that last experience I strolled down to the river one afternoon to wait for the boat from Dajabon. It was so hot that I took off my sun-helmet and laid it in the grass beside me. On the arrival of the boat, I picked up my helmet again and was about to put it on when the jungle instinct sent a danger signal stabbing through my brain. I flung the hat quickly away. In the sweat-band, between the corks, lay a finger-long scorpion, his poison-dealing sting projecting like a violet-blue dagger. That episode might have been the end of me.

"Of late I have even taken care to scrutinize the ground before I pick anything up. You can see that the ever-threatening dangers of the jungle must develop a fatalistic tendency in a man. Death stalks him in many ways: in the fang of a snake; an offended native may mix poison in one's drink; a million malaria-carrying insects swarm everywhere; sudden equatorial floods may capsize the boat. Not one, but a thousand different deaths lurk in the forest. The end is always near and always comes unannounced.

"Only the strongest will and the most unwavering determination can survive in such a life, where every day is a ceaseless and unavailing struggle against death: a struggle that can never be won. There is no victory over the jungle, just a delay of the inevitable. One day, when a man is least prepared, the end comes; the jungle wins. . . ."

Hickman laughed bitterly. "I have grown old in this fight,

but I wouldn't have missed it for anything. All the same I'm damned glad to get a little news of the world beyond."

His speech changed suddenly from soft, slow German to a harsh Yankee twang. "That's why I took the opportunity of inviting you to my shack. I knew days ago that you were coming here and it wasn't your negroes that told me. My servants got the news from somewhere and passed it on to me. You were watched the whole time without knowing it. Didn't I tell you the jungle never sleeps!"

A cunning flicker of laughter creased his face. That hackneyed sentence about the jungle never sleeping seemed to amuse him. The smell of the neat rum which the old man was pouring into my glass was stimulating. It dispelled the mildewed atmosphere that hung about the room, and as I lifted the glass to my lips a grateful, fiery warmth flowed into me. When Hickman leant back again in his chair I had an opportunity of studying his face.

His eyes were hypnotic, bluish-gray, with restless, stabbing pupils that glared like two black pin-heads out of his dark, leathery face. In spite of the hardness of his glance there was no life in it; it seemed almost as though the spirit behind the eyes had long since been quenched. I was beginning to feel uneasy under his piercing gaze. What sort of a man was this? Was he quite sane or was he mad?

Here in the jungle anything was possible. Anything could happen. What had I in common with this white man who had voluntarily chosen to spend his whole life entirely severed from civilization? I made a frantic effort to get up, but my muscles refused to respond. There was no escape. I could only sit and think and see. . . .

A swarm of insects were humming round the lamp, singeing their wings, and threatening every moment to extinguish the flame as they fell in hundreds down the milky glass chimney. If the lamp should go out while this man sat staring at me . . .

Emerald-green lizards zigzagged across the walls, or hung head downwards from the ceiling snapping at flies. Across one corner stretched a vast spider's web and on it crouched a fat, black hairy spider winding her twitching victim in a silken cocoon preparatory to eating it.

Like a breath of madness the idea swept across me. The old man was himself a poisonous spider in whose web *I* was caught. He was mad—at any moment he might be seized with homicidal mania. My heart pounded until it almost choked me as I realized how helplessly alone and unprotected I was. Even supposing the man was sane, what would happen to me if I caught malaria or the dreaded beri-beri? . . .

I pulled myself together, trying to think of cleaner and pleasanter things. Nervously I questioned and cross-questioned Hickman about life in the settlement, the weather, trade, connections with the outer world . . . anything to stave off the awful silence that might fall.

The man seemed to be unaware of the spiritual and bodily anguish that was torturing me. He was content to enjoy the rare pleasure of another white man's company. I tried to realize this and to force myself, with every atom of willpower I possessed, to be just to him, to believe that he was really only a harmless old crank. Every now and then I shook myself, determined to ward off an overpowering desire for sleep and to keep my brain clear from the mists of unreasoning terror that swept across it.

Hickman's extraordinary quiet and lassitude started the fancy in my brain that all spirit and power had long ago deserted the shriveled old body. I was looking at a ghost—a soulless figure of skin and bone. It required a great mental effort to pull myself together and follow the conversation when Hickman started off again: "In spite of our seclusion there is, when the rainy season permits, a lively traffic up and down the river in timber, cotton, tobacco, coffee, and cocoa.

"We've got some first-rate sport here too. All you need to do is pick up your gun, walk out of the house, and there's your shoot in front of you, full of musk-hogs and birds. I always manage to have some fresh meat at table. Long ago I used to hunt through the forest with my son. A fine boy he was. He died one day in this room. The yellow fever got him. . . ."

The old man's voice trembled slightly. I knew now. He wasn't mad, not dead to the world; he still felt pain and sorrow. In some strange way I was glad of that, for it showed me that I had a man opposite me and no ghost. But it was a man now turned to stone. A man whose shadow sat grim and threatening, no more alive but dead. He was a *corpse.* I could have screamed with terror; sweat oozed in great drops from every pore, wetting my clothes till they stuck clammily to my skin. The fetid air clogged my lungs. My breath came in thick, short gasps. A fit of vomiting seized me and I stumbled to the window and leant out, panting for fresh, cool air that was not to be had.

I felt enwrapped by a strange sensation that came out of the fathomless depths of the jungle. Something weird and mysterious pulled toward me.

At first I thought—"It must be my own pulse beating loud and fiercely through my veins." But that was madness.

I groaned with terror—of course I had no heart. *My* heart was beating out there alone, somewhere in the jungle—beating and beating, madly and relentlessly.

There it was again—and again. It boomed hollowly and quivered through the heavy swamp air. It was almost inaudible now. I writhed under the torture.

Something deep down and irresistible held me in thrall—I was listening to my own blood. Hark!—a new and wilder rhythm was drumming through my body. A rhythm that raised me to the height of exultation—and cast me down to weak-kneed helplessness. And then lifted me up again on a wave of omnipotence, changing me to a rampant beast of the jungle.

I was standing in the open now.

There was no resistance possible. In complete surrender I stumbled on towards the summoning beat.

My fear was long since past.

Only the mighty power of the rhythm gave me strength to walk. Now right, now left; it seemed as if I had known the way since time began as I brushed like a shadow through the thickets. Mustn't think—not think; only listen, listen. . . .

Nearer and nearer. The thick bushes crashed under my plunging body which neither felt thorns nor whipping branches.

All at once I stopped dead, wild-eyed. In front of me roared a blazing fire.

The secret was mine.

Round the fire squatted a ghostly circle of naked men. On the far side there was a gap in the ring where hung the giant drums; hollowed-out tree trunks stretched with goat skin, which resounded under the nimble fingers and wrists of their shadowy musicians.

I ran forward and squatted down amongst the black spectators. In the center of the circle were the dancers, men and women, their satiny torsos glistening crimson in the ruddy glow of the flames. They moved slowly round the fire, stamping their straddled legs in time to the beat of the drums. They moved slowly—but with devilish intensity and power, straining every muscle till the sweat poured down their bodies. Their faces were distorted with the effort. Here were no kindly natives, but lustful, dancing dervishes.

Tom-ti-ti-tom——

Tom-titi-tom——

The drums took on a different rhythm, rattling out a sharp staccato message, accompanied by the heavy pounding of the bass. Faster and faster flew the feet of the dancers as they whirled round the fire. Their smooth muscles writhed and cramped as under the blows of an invisible whip; but a whip whose lashes were caresses, exciting and maddening their animal desires.

"Eeeh—yah—eeh—yah——"

Shrill screams burst out from their throats, rending the heavy monotone of the drums. The night shivered with the falsetto yells.

In the center of the dancers the slim, smooth body of a girl sprang up with arms raised high above her head. Stark naked like the others, except for a narrow string of shells about her hips, she swayed there, dull lights glancing off her ebony skin. Her waving hair, crowned with a white orchid, cascaded down about her oval head, framing a face of almost Caucasian beauty.

In her expression shone the ancient fires of Africa.

Her body was gorgeous. Two passionate eyes gleaming through the soft long lashes; teeth like pearls shining between blood-red lips; breasts carved from black translucent alabaster.

As she danced her body seemed two disconnected halves; below—the slender, wide-spread legs firmly implanted on the ground; above—smooth as an eel from the hips upward, her body writhed like an angry snake, moving in a wild frenzy, faster and faster in an orgasm of transcendent ecstasy.

"Yip—yip—yip"—a piercing scream burst from her frothing mouth.

"Boola—boola," echoed a choir of broad, metallic voices.

These were love songs; sung under the starshine in a forest clearing, embodying all the joys and the sufferings, all the romance and the pathos of life. They spoke of submission to the monstrous spirit of the jungle, of the dread and sorrow of living and being; a crying out of the inmost soul. Tears and sobs, fears and hopes, happiness and rejoicing, woven together in the haunting melody of the drums.

The dance was reaching its climax.

The urge of occult, primitive powers possessed me, making me one with the dancers, a part of the forest, of Nature herself.

Just to stay here. Nothing more. . . .

Two flaming eyes met mine and held me in thrall. Like a slow, slinking panther the dancer came near, quite near to me. Her gaze pierced my brain. Giddiness swirled in my head. Everything became dark; darker and darker in the mists. . . .

I closed my eyes.

A heavy scent, sweet as fermenting honey or hot opium, pressed over me, clouding my senses. It was the white orchid in her blue-black hair. Already I felt the heat of her body. The blood was coursing in my cheeks.

Hot breath whispered sweetly; an unutterably tender voice murmured in my ears.

"Shall I dance for you, white man—for you alone? White men are beautiful, so beautiful."

Gently her fingers stroked across my cheek. Her presence soothed me and a sense of boundless weariness pressed me down . . . down. . . .

I heard heavy, stumbling steps and a harsh drunken voice shouting.

The soothing finger-tips were gone. I opened my eyes. Above me towered Hickman's bony figure. The girl was talking to him, pressed close to his body and stroking his leathery face with her delicate fingers.

"Shall we sleep?" she whispered.

My body craved water with an overpowering thirst, but a thirst for more than water roused me from my torpor. I heard Hickman's rough voice, coming from a great distance:

"Come back with me to the house. It's not wise to listen to these drums of the jungle."

I staggered to my feet and hung on to his arm. He gave me a gentle push in the direction of the settlement.

"My daughter here will make up a bed for you."

He tried to laugh and a thousand furrows and wrinkles seamed his face, but there was no laughter in his staring eyes.

His voice rang hoarsely in my ears.

"Yes, this is my daughter."

He said no more. Between the two of them I stumbled back

to the hut. The roar of the drums still echoed through my head, pursuing me. "There is no escape."

My teeth chattered with fever.

Sleep—only to sleep. . . .

VI. MON REPOS

A WEEK ago I moved into a palace.

A real palace, with a wide flight of steps up to the front entrance and a reception room and an audience room and scores of other apartments great and small. In front of the house was a broad expanse of unkempt grass which evidently had once been a lawn and still showed sign of garden architecture; and in the middle of the lawn lay a muddy, ornamental pond with a fountain rising out of the shallow stone basin. But it was long years since any water had spouted from those bronze mouths and the floor of the basin was overgrown with weeds through which swam all kinds of crawling and creeping creatures.

The palace demesne was surrounded by a high stone wall, one section of which bordered a little native village. The only admittance was through a lovely old pair of wrought-iron gates under a scroll of flourishing letters which said:

MON REPOS

A haven of rest; and just what I needed.

An attack of malaria had forced me to leave as quickly as possible the unhealthful, fever-haunted region of the Massacre River, and thus I came, by boat, horse, and car, to Port-au-Prince, the capital of Haiti. I was met there by Andresen Jensen, a New York friend of mine whom I had known for years and whom I had frequently met in all parts of the old and new worlds. He had been born a Dane and at an early age had wandered out into the world. For thirty years he had traveled the two Americas, acquainting himself with all the countries and peoples between Punta Arenas and Hudson Bay. The last time I had seen him was in New York, in an artists' haunt called "The Blue Ribbon Restaurant," when he had made me promise that I would visit Haiti and stay with him on the plantation where he was manager.

So I was now fulfilling my promise and I was enjoying myself. To be with Jensen meant to be up and doing! We rode off in the early morning just after the sun had risen and began by inspecting some outlying plantation; then we went along to supervise the weighing of cotton bales or the construction of a new irrigation scheme; followed by a visit to the mayor of some distant village to pay taxes that had become due; and in the evening we had various social duties to perform. I saw a great deal of Haiti during my stay with Jensen for he was always traveling backwards and forwards across the island. At last I got tired of his continual restlessness and I told him plainly that I wanted to settle down in some place where I could have a little peace and quiet and jot down my various experiences.

"Why don't you go to 'Mon Repos'?" he suggested. "No one will disturb you there, not even the great god Damballa himself."

The rather funereal name of the house accorded perfectly with my present mood, so I agreed. The same day found Jensen and myself driving out to Bizóton to inspect the property. Twenty-four hours later I moved in, bag and baggage, complete with hammock, mosquito net, painting equipment, and, last but not least, a banjo.

An imposing avenue of royal palms, a hundred and fifty years old, led from the iron gates to the wide portico, while behind the building lay a grove of trees bordering the beach and the blue Antilles Sea. This estate, which really showed great taste and sense of beauty, had originally been owned by a Spanish nobleman, the master of a hundred slaves, whose name has long since been forgotten. It then became the summer residence of Florville Hipolyte, the negro president. Hipolyte had been an infamous adherent of Voodoo and when he died they found a woman's skeleton in his bedroom cupboard. Then, after one of the numerous revolutions which usually coincided with the bankruptcy of the republic, the estate was presented in default of cash payment to the English owners of Jensen's plantation; and thus my friend was able to place the palace at my disposal.

First of all I explored the interior of the building.

My footsteps echoed through the empty rooms and on the rickety staircases, raising thick clouds of malodorous dust. Nothing would have persuaded me to sleep alone in this rambling empty house, so I inspected the garden for a suitable place to sling my hammock. I eventually discovered, in the center of the palm grove, a charming little summer house which I entered for a closer scrutiny. Unfortunately the inside was far from charming for it was very much inhabited.

As soon as I stepped across the threshold a guardian lizard streaked out between my legs. Up in the roof I espied another unwelcome dweller. A snake, coiled round a crossbeam overhead, gave vent to her rage at my disturbing her fruitful lizard hunt by a vicious hissing and flickering of the tongue. Carefully I tabulated the result of my inspection. The list of tropical discomforts ranged from scorpions to three-inch millipedes. Fat spiders, warty toads, squeaking mice, and a battalion of scurrying cockroaches completed the zoölogical decorations. The place was too crowded for comfort.

In the course of my hasty retreat I realized why the hut was so overpopulated. The roof was made of thatched palm leaves which offered a desirable breeding place for cockroaches and other crawling beasts. The start of a perfect sequence of causation, for the cockroaches ate the palm leaves, the lizards ate the cockroaches, the snakes ate the lizards, and who ate the snakes I didn't dare to think!

I looked round the garden for a little longer and then decided to sling my hammock between two palm trees about a hundred yards from the house.

Evening came and faded into night. I crept like a contortionist beneath the mosquito net and into my airy bed. In a moment I was fast asleep.

CRASH!! I sat bolt upright. . . . A rotting palm had fallen to the ground, throwing a few scared birds into the air who squawked angrily. At last they settled down in another tree and silence reigned.

The disturbance had shaken my nerves and I wondered anxiously what would happen next. I did not have long to wait for I had scarcely closed my eyes when through the darkness came a cry—hollow and terrible.

"Wuh—wuh—ha—ha—ha——"

Good God! What was that? The noise came from the house; there was no doubt about it—the palace *was* haunted.

Thoroughly scared I rolled out of the hammock, switched on my flashlight, and advanced cautiously. When I reached the wall of the house I heard it again: "Wuh—wuh—ha—ha—ha——" That came from just round the corner. The shrieking monster must be in the porch. I crept along the wall and up the broad steps. At the top all was silent. I lit up every corner with my light but there was nothing to be seen; just the bare stone floor covered with dust. Suddenly the noise started again, this time immediately behind me. My scalp prickled and I was so overcome with terror that I was unable to move. There was a long agonizing moment of inaction and then I swung round. At first I thought the floor was bare. No—there was something in the corner. My light picked it out. It was a huge frog, fat and swollen like a mango, hopping across the floor and uttering its strange love-call: "Wuh—wuh—ha—ha——"

Cursing my foolish alarm I returned to bed, though not without some nimble sidesprings caused by inexplicable rustlings in the grass. The night resumed its peaceful sway; everything was quiet and still. But I could not get to sleep, and in order to be prepared for any new emergency that might arise I laid the torch under the pillow on my right-hand side and the revolver on my left.

Finally I dozed off and I suppose I must have been asleep about two hours when I suddenly woke up again. I was bathed in sweat and could scarcely breathe. Something was pressing heavily on my chest. With a superhuman effort I sat up. The animal, for I knew it was alive by its breathing, sprang lightly to the ground. I fumbled wildly for my torch in the darkness and it fell out of the hammock into the long grass. Vainly I strained my eyes and groped about to find it. It was lost till the morning. I was condemned to remain in the dark, and there, not two feet away from me, were two glowing eyes, which held mine in their hypnotic stare. "By heavens!" I thought, "a *tiger*."

At any rate I still had the revolver. I gripped it. Now . . . steady . . . With feverish agitation, and still half asleep, my hand wobbled in a palsy of fear. I was absolutely alone, under the shadow of a house which had cloaked the nameless orgies of a Voodoo President. I thought wildly of frogs and snakes and ghosts . . . shut my eyes tight and tugged at the trigger.

Bang!!! The revolver went off and the bullet nearly hit a large cat which had combined a nocturnal mousing prowl from the village with a short nap on my heroic breast!

The dawning day slowly dispelled the ghost-haunted darkness of that terrible night.

I took my morning bath in the sea beneath the palm trees. On the beach lay the palm that had inaugurated my hours of tribulation. Its top was submerged beneath the water and its roots pointed helplessly to the sky. Thousands of ants scurried along the trunk, loaded with eggs and larvae, carrying their precious burdens ashore to safety. Hurrying from the land came thousands more, returning to complete the work of rescue. Some cockroaches lay on the log, but they proved no obstacle to the industrious insects who either ran over them or pushed them to one side. Mercilessly the tide crept higher and higher, until at last a frothing wavelet broke over the remnants of the ruined insect city, drowning the helpless little ones together with their brave rescuers and the sluggard cockroaches.

Now that the night was over I had to busy myself with domestic arrangements, so I went into the village to look round for servants. I was soon successful. Faustin, a smart-looking lad, and Yvonne, a pretty little black girl, offered their services for two gourdes a day.

Yvonne was a first-rate cook. She provided meals exclusively composed of things that grew and lived within the palace domains. Hors d'œuvres came from the sea—oysters and mussels. The solution to the soup problem was to be found behind the house in the lagoon—a turtle. After that came wild pigeon and ducks caught by Faustin in ingeniously contrived traps. Potatoes could be had in armfuls for the mere trouble of bending down and gathering them up. Along the hedge beside the garden wall grew the substance of a thousand tapioca puddings to which cocoanuts supplied the milk. The juice of the cocoanuts was as good as the best cow's milk, only not quite so creamy. As dessert bananas, oranges, and mangoes grew in profusion. Drinks were supplied by Yvonne's mother who brewed excellent palm wine, while for those of a teetotal persuasion it was easy enough to make fresh lemon squash. In the evening I had a cup of delicious coffee, roasted from wild beans and sweetened with juice of sugar cane and I always filled my pipe with dried tobacco leaves of my own picking—"Mon Repos" brand!

Yvonne's face had lighted up proudly when I praised her thrifty housekeeping and she immediately proceeded to shake the necessary crockery down from the trees. Broad, dried palm leaves served as a tablecloth and serviettes. The plates were cut from wood, and the halves of cocoanut shells made excellent cups. A hollowed-out gourd held the wine, and knives and forks were carved from bamboo sticks.

In the garden of "Mon Repos" I enjoyed the best and tastiest meals of my life.

Faustin was a willing and intelligent servant, but in one respect he remained incorrigible. He could not understand why his Haitian ideas of what constituted cleanliness should offend me. Once I caught him cleaning a spoon with his saliva-moistened "handkerchief." With truly Christian patience I tried to teach him better. But he looked at me in a puzzled way and turned round and blew the dust off a plate. I left him to his own devices. On the next day I found him drying the crockery with his loin cloth. . . .

Thenceforth I did the washing-up myself.

Yet in many other respects Faustin was of an inquiring turn of mind and ready to learn. In course of time he became so attached to me that it was difficult to get rid of him. He followed me like a shadow.

One evening at sunset I was sitting on the back veranda of the palace enjoying the wonderful view over the sea, Faustin as usual squatting beside me chewing. All at once he looked up and asked me why I was looking at the sky. I tried to show him the beauties that lay in a tropical sunset, but he only shook his woolly head and said it was scarcely worth troubling about a thing that could be seen every evening.

Then he wanted to know what the clouds were made of. My explanation—that clouds were water-vapor—failed to satisfy him. He shook his head again and said: "Anyone can see that that's land up in the sky. Look—there are mountains and valleys and seas."

When Faustin's brain began working the novelty was manifested all over his body. His eyes squinted, his thick lips moved as if he were holding silent communion with himself, and his fingers opened and shut convulsively. On these occasions I left him alone until he was ready to speak and catechize me further.

"See here," he went on, describing a wide circle with his arm, "so big is the earth. From there—" he pointed to the sea's horizon, "—comes a ship. Only a few white men walk out of the ship, so the land of the white men must be small. There aren't many white men, are there? Else more would come here."

He placed his elbows on his knees, and with his face between his hands he smiled at me triumphantly.

"The world is so big, Faustin," I answered, "that we can only see a very little bit of it. Beyond the horizon are many great countries, with rivers so broad that you couldn't swim across them; with mountains so high that you could never reach the top; and with forests so wide that you never come to the end of them."

Faustin listened to me breathlessly, his eyes rolling with astonishment. Then he asked me which land I came from. I told him that my native city was Vienna, far away in Europe. I explained to him that to get there one could travel in either of two directions: towards the sunrise or towards the sunset. He could not grasp this amazing contradiction, so I took a grapefruit and showed him how the world revolves round the sun.

"Once a day?" he asked.

"Yes," I replied.

There was a moment's pause while this new aspect of creation sank into his brain. Then he said:

"Why?"

I gave it up because I could not answer that one myself.

The next morning Faustin cleared the pond of weeds and I turned on the fountains. I then invited all the children in the village to come and have a free bath. They came in dozens and filled the water to overflowing with their sprawling brown bodies.

Yvonne crawled out of the mêlée and flung herself dripping at my feet. As she lay there, her body gleaming like a mirror in the sun, she began improvising a little song which she chanted in swinging rhythm. The words of the song were not exactly *spirituel* and they certainly did not rhyme, but the chorus in the bath gave the refrain a forceful rendering.

The smaller ones imitated their elders by singing and shouting and squeaking. They started a rhythmic accompaniment to the music by beating their hands on their wet thighs. Some little devils seemed to prefer slapping the hindquarters of others to their own. This was a signal for general hooliganism. Each pushed the other into the water, head first or feet first, whichever was the easiest. And so the afternoon passed in shouting and laughter until nightfall put an end to the revelries.

One sunny morning I rolled from my hammock and tripped over a brown body lying underneath me on the grass. It was Faustin. Beside him lay another little boy who sat up and rubbed his eyes.

"What on earth are you doing here?" I asked.

"Me?" he answered, with exaggerated innocence. "I was waiting for you, sir."

"And you?" I addressed the other lad.

"I—I've been waiting with Faustin," he stammered.

Faustin tried to distract my attention and put me in a good humor by climbing up a cocoanut tree. He stuck his toes into the bark and clambered up the sloping trunk as agilely as a monkey. When he got up to the top he pitched the huge nuts—crash—crash—into the wet grass beside me. I chose the largest specimen and removed the husk by slitting it lengthwise with the machete. Then I hammered in the "eye," but not quite skillfully enough to prevent the milk squirting out all over my face—which sent the boys into paroxysms of laughter.

Faustin and Yvonne always looked on when I was working

at my black and white illustrations. They quietly squatted down on each side of me and watched every movement of my hand. On this particular morning Faustin announced that he was always going to be my servant and was coming back with me to Europe.

"But, Faustin," I said, looking at him earnestly, "I've got to go back to America first."

"What!" he screamed. "Back to the *États Unis* where they burn negroes!"

After that he changed his mind about accompanying me.

A little later I felt thirsty and asked him to fetch me a glass of lemonade. The drink soon arrived, but it was not Faustin who brought it. A strange child whom I had never seen before held the glass in his grimy paws. He watched me silently while I drank and then he announced that it was his name-day and he would be grateful for a small tip. I could not refuse this polite request so I gave him a coin.

Great was my astonishment when, a few days later, the same little good-for-nothing arrived with another glass of lemonade. He informed me that it was again his name-day and demanded the customary reward.

"What! Today as well? Have you got a name-day every week?" I asked in horror.

"Yes, master," came the disconcerting reply, "I'm called Friday!"

To the negro a white man seems just as strange and different as does the negro to the European. Yvonne told me once she could not understand why the white ladies wore thick clothes all day and undressed at night. She developed her thesis by saying: "In the night when it's cold we negroes put on warm clothes, but during the daytime, when the sun shines, we take everything off."

I smiled to myself. The child was right.

Sometimes I had other guests to watch me working. One day when Yvonne had just gone to visit her mother in the village, I wanted a letter posted, so I sent Faustin with it to Port-au-Prince. He did postman for me in typical Haitian fashion. He placed the letter on his woolly head and "fastened" it there with half a brick; then he trotted off. At last I was alone and could really get down to work.

Suddenly I had the feeling that I was not alone. I glanced up. In Heaven's name what nightmare creature was that standing by my elbow? Of all creeping, crawling, and flying animals, what label did the zoölogists hang on this one?

Its stumpy green wings fluffed out like short skirts round the hips of a prima ballerina and its weird triangular-shaped head hung on the end of a neck as thin as a piece of string. The apparition waggled its horrid head at me and nodded pensively every time I moved. At the extremities of its arms were, not hands, but crooked, hairy claws, shaped like boat hooks. Neither of us seemed to please the other, so the animal turned its back on me and waddled to the side of the table where it raised its claws as if in fervent prayer. Then it spread its little skirt out and, with a loud hiss, vanished.

Immediately after this I had another strange spectator. A sustained and angry whirring announced a large cockroach which settled on my sketching block just where I had that minute painted a bright blue sky. Showing no respect for my work of art, the Goliath insect paddled about in the wet ultramarine, and, since he seemed a rare specimen, I let him be.

He was almost the size of my hand, with two wings the

color of tempered steel folded over a red-striped body. On the armor-plating of his back Nature had splashed, in modernistic mood, bright spots of yellow.

The strangest thing about him was his forelegs which were so long that they kept getting continually tangled up in his four hinder ones. All the time he was settled on my block there came a furious humming from him that sounded like a miniature sawmill.

He wandered backwards and forwards about half a dozen times across the painting, and every now and again his feeble legs knocked together and his head nodded just like an old grandfather pondering the futility of life.

Finally he fell off the table and was lost in the wilderness of grass at my feet.

One day, during a tropical downpour, I was sitting in a room in the palace working and I suddenly heard the sound of a loud kiss. I looked round in astonishment because I knew I was alone in the house. There it was again—*tschik, tschak*—the same kissing noise only this time coming from the ceiling. Who could be greeting me so tenderly? I examined the beams overhead and noticed on one of them a little green object moving about, but that was surely far too small for such a large noise. *Tschik-tschak . . . tschik-tschak.* It was by no means an unpleasant sound; indeed it was just like a good, hearty kiss, such as I have sometimes heard coming from the top of a haystack or the inside of a barn. The little green object up above moved along the beam about a yard and was quickly joined by another one, and then by hundreds more until the whole ceiling teemed with tiny lizards. Two of them fought heatedly over a wasp and forgot for the moment that they were hanging upside-down. They both fell into my lap with half a wasp in each mouth. I quickly threw a rag over them (a smacking kiss came from my lap!), then gently lifted one corner and peeped in. My sole trophy was a lizard's tail; its owner had long since vanished. It seemed cruel, but I was comforted by the thought that the poor creature would soon grow a new tail.

When work was over, I usually sat on the veranda and dozed. I found that on this "Island of the Winds," a land where time seemed half forgotten, my thoughts always turned to the trivial, unimportant things in life. I remembered a story told me by Bouk, the chemist, in Port-au-Prince. It was about an old German professor who for two years wandered backwards and forwards across the island with his butterfly net and killing box, catching all the hundreds of different insects that he came across. He returned home and took exactly eight years cataloguing his collection and preparing it for a museum. What a moral could be drawn from that!

From the veranda I had a wonderful view into the distance. To my right lay the violet outline of Gonave Island, shadowed against the deep blue of the sky beyond. Behind the island, stretching from north to south as far as the eye could see, lay the Windward Passage, the great highway of sea traffic between North and South America.

Ships of all sizes and sorts, cargo boats, liners, tankers, and sailing vessels, loomed up over the far horizon, crossed my field of vision, and vanished down the rim of the sea again. Many of the steamers only revealed their presence by a traveling column of smoke; the ships themselves were over the edge and out of sight.

Whither bound?

Southwards—to the glorious, the most wonderful harbor in the world, Rio de Janeiro; or to Santos, or to Buenos Aires, the great city on the river Plate, or even round the treacherous Horn?

And northwards—to the Bermudas, to New York, to Quebec? Or perhaps they were heading for the tropical lands of Central America; Mexico, Guatemala, Costa Rica, Honduras, the Panama Canal, maybe one amongst them was bound for the country where I spent my student days, Germany.

Germany—how far away and how different!

Yvonne often kept me company on those dreamy evenings. She was not so talkative as Faustin, but to make up for her lack of inquisitiveness she sang unceasingly. This recital to which I became an involuntary audience was far from melodious, but on the other hand her voice was not unpleasing. Most of the time she sat on the ground and drew in the sand cabalistic figures like those used for Voodoo ritual, a knowledge probably gained from her mother who was the local Mamaloi.

Nothing, not even Yvonne, could disturb the perfect peace of those evenings on the veranda. During the day it was fairly quiet there, except for the continual hum of insects; but in the evening, directly seven o'clock had struck, there began a most unusual symphonic concert.

Scarcely had the hands of my wrist-watch reached the hour, when a silence fell, followed almost immediately by an introductory andante issuing as from a choir of hoarse clarionets. This lasted for a minute or two and was then augmented by a crescendo humming. Lastly a deafening chorus of innumerable frogs struck up the tune. From here, from there, from every corner, came the penetrating croak which quickly rose to such a volume that it became impossible to carry on any conversation. The noise was reminiscent of mid-day in the middle of New York. There, in the city, was the din of the elevated railway and hooting motor cars; here, amidst the jungle, were the myriad manifestations of tropical life calling to each other "good-night"—or was it, perhaps, "good-morning?"

At half-past seven a sudden hush fell, just as though Nature had rapped with her conductor's baton, reducing her disharmonious orchestra to silence. Once or twice came the screeching of a parrot from the distant branches. Then complete silence—and Mon Repos slept.

Overhead the heavens arched in an infinite deep blue canopy studded with golden spangles. Low on the horizon shone the Pole star. Directly above me three unwinking planets gleamed—red Mars on top, below him the giant Jupiter, and lowest of all, setting in her resplendent glory, was lovely Venus. The Great Wagon lay overturned, shafts pointing downwards. To my right towered the Southern Cross, and far above all, like a hidden mystery, the Milky Way stretched in a luminous ribbon across the celestial zenith.

The sea splashed on the sandy beach in eternal unchanging rhythm.

The last evening of my stay at "Mon Repos" I spent in the little negro village outside the walls. I brought my banjo and played it for the amusement of my black friends and they thoroughly enjoyed themselves. On every face was laughter and happiness as men and women swayed in time to the beat of the jazz. Little naked babies clustered round, laid their woolly heads in my lap, rolled over me, climbed up me, and altogether so encumbered me that I could scarcely move my arms.

I changed to a Viennese love song.

Just as the wild beat of modern jazz had made them happy, sweeping away their cares, so now the soft lilting tune held them spellbound and silent, gazing into the distance. . . .

As dusk fell I left the hospitable village and took a stroll through the park of my domain. It was a perfect night. On the beach I passed a young couple and I stepped aside into the shadow of the trees to avoid disturbing them.

It was almost dark now and one of the two lit a dried banana branch and held it aloft as a torch. It was Faustin, the young devil, arm in arm with Yvonne!

Grotesquely distorted shadows danced on the trees; then faded as the light retreated and disappeared.

VII. POLYCHROMATA

Port-au-Prince.

THE capital of Haiti stretches in a broad half-moon along the shores of the Gulf of Gonaves. Down below at water level, sweltering in the tropical heat, lies the Old Town, comprising the harbor, native quarters, and government buildings and cemetery; while up above, on the cool slopes of the surrounding hills, live the black élite of Haiti and the white residents. The handsome lime-washed villas stand in gardens of incomparable beauty, with smooth green lawns, brilliant flower-beds, and little palm groves, each encircled by a high stone wall.

Such a paradise of rest and quietude was my friend Jensen's property, lying on the way to Pétionville, the most select suburb of Port-au-Prince. From the road nothing could be seen of the estate for it was entirely surrounded by a ten-foot wall; but on passing through a high door in this wall one came into a circular park in the middle of which lay the villa. The whole aspect of verdant lawns, ornamental terraces, trees, and fountains gave the impression of a medieval pleasure garden. An avenue of royal palms bordered the winding drive and near the house, on the right, was an open-air swimming bath with water spouting from a bronze gargoyle. The villa itself was built in the style of a French château, with balconies and broad verandas on three sides of it. Next to the house and slightly behind it was a medley of long, low buildings; the stables and coach-houses. Immediately behind the further wall of the park lay an arm of the jungle stretching down from the mountains as if to devour this green and white paradise in its insatiable maw.

The place was perfect. So might a rich colonist of the slaving era have lived, surrounded with the best and richest that tropical nature could give. Actually, Jensen told me, a former president of the republic had built the house for his pretty young mulatto mistress. I thought to myself that the old man had certainly shown good taste in choosing such a perfect setting for his love-nest, and I was grateful to him for the incomparable beauty of the place and its glorious view over seas and mountains such as the Riviera could never hope to rival.

Jensen, who was a bachelor, thought it incumbent upon him to restore the old tradition of the villa, and during my stay there he installed a young Creole from San Domingo as mistress of the house. She was a fine girl of exceptional intelligence, for besides her mother tongue, Spanish, she spoke French, Creole, and English.

Jensen and I got on extremely well together for the simple reason that we agreed upon almost every subject. Nevertheless we often held heated arguments about the most diverse topics, such as monogamy and polygamy, Mussolini and the Five Year Plan, Kokoschka's portraits, the Polish Corridor, and the future of the talkies! Jensen, who was of a very excitable nature, would become scarlet in the face whenever the discussion reached an *impasse* and would then terminate it by remarking gloomily: "Every artist has a screw loose somewhere!"

"Tropical choler," said Blass, the secretary, who was frequently present at these post-prandial controversies; and Señorita Hellas would come in with some glasses of iced "swizzles" and restore peace with her happy laughter.

Jensen let me ride his horses whenever I wished, and this permission came in very useful, enabling me to explore thoroughly the neighborhood of Port-au-Prince and the town itself. I usually left the house immediately after breakfast and trotted off down the steep Rue Lalue in search of new adventures and encounters.

The scenes and incidents that I met with in my daily ride were so numerous and diverse, and followed one another with such rapidity, that I could never have recorded all of them, even with the aid of a camera. I will however try to describe some of the episodes that struck me as being most unusual or amusing and consequently have remained longest in my memory. It is probable that I experienced much that was more interesting and more important than what I have set down here, but nevertheless the memories that remain will,

I hope, draw an adequate and colorful picture of this strange harbor of the Antilles. . . .

Directly outside the garden gate the bright panorama of every-day working life began. I cleft my way through an unending stream of loafing, running, screaming, laughing, black-skinned men and women carrying huge colored bundles on their heads. Naked children chased one another through the crowds of travelers or lay on the road in the shadow of the palms kicking up the dust with their feet. Diminutive mules trotted along laden with enormous packages on top of which like a mountain on a mouse perched a fat, black "Mammy" who passed the time smoking her stumpy pipe and belaboring her wretched beast of burden.

All faces were turned to the town. It was market day, and men, women, and children walked slowly down the hill, grunting under their heavy loads and the scorching heat of the sun. Yet in spite of the discomfort, nothing would have persuaded them to sell their goods by the wayside because then they would have no excuse for going into the market, for greeting their friends, for gossiping, bargaining, laughing, shouting, and quarreling; and they had been looking forward to that for a whole week!

My way led me past rows of primitive mud huts, where the women squatted over the gutter and washed their clothes amidst a volley of lively chattering. In front of almost every hut were goods displayed for sale on an upturned chest. But I never saw anyone make a purchase and the saleswomen (that is, where there were any) dozed peacefully in the dark shadow of their huts.

The shimmering heat became ever fiercer the lower I descended into the valley. My horse, a typical Haitian nag of small build, stopped motionless every quarter of an hour

She waggled her ears pensively and let her head sink down and down until she began to utter gentle snores. I let her sleep for a few minutes. Then I stuck my spurs into her flanks and "Rosie," as she was called, awoke refreshed for another short trot.

Once in the town I was soon lost in a maze of narrow, winding alleys. In the shadow of a doorway sat two negresses, combing each other's hair. Through the open window behind I saw another negress with a corn-cob pipe in her mouth, who squatted on the ground and turned an antique sewing-machine. A few sailors sat at the tables outside the "Café Guadeloupe" playing cards. Next door a fish shop exhaled its overpowering odor. A shark hung from a hook and a boy was slitting its belly open. The entrails oozed out and fell on the pavement. Beggars wrapped in filthy rags hobbled through the streets exposing their festering sores as they begged for alms. In the harbor a ship was unloading. There was no need for machinery here for all the work was done by hurrying black legs and sweating bodies. Under the eagle eye of a blasphemous overseer, long lines of fuzzy-headed natives emerged heavy-laden from the hold and returned from the warehouse empty handed to vanish again into the yawning waist of the ship.

"Why don't you use trucks?" I asked the overseer.

"But, monsieur," he answered, "think of the number of honest men who would be unemployed if we unloaded with trucks! We've got plenty of workers and we use them all and they're all happy."

There was no challenging that argument.

In the center of a throng of jumping children stood an old gray-haired negro who was performing on an asthmatic concertina. From the open window of a large building on my left came a penetrating noise as of a swarm of bees. Someone informed me it was a school, so I steered my mount alongside the wall and peeped into the classroom. I must have made a clatter as I pulled myself up to the window ledge, for the attention and eyes of the pupils swung with one accord from their teacher to me. The latter was the last to see me, but when he did he advanced on the window with such a threatening expression that I hastily vanished round the corner. In response to my urgency "Rosie" nearly tripped over an *al fresco* restaurant which its proprietress, an obese negress, had set up with great success right in the middle of the road. The customers were mostly dock hands who sat round on the pavement and on packing cases, gobbling their lunches. The "restaurant" consisted of a large enamel saucepan full of "Port-au-Prince stew," beside which rose a stack of big round discs looking exactly like yellow straw hats with the brims taken off. Actually the discs were slices of cassava, a kind of native bread. When a customer ordered his luncheon, "Mammy" smeared a ladleful of stew on to one of these edible plates which disappeared together with the meat into the gourmet's stomach. By this economical device she saved herself both the cost of plates and the trouble of washing up.

Coming along the street a little girl cried her wares in a high, piping voice: "Kola—kola—kola!" (Creole for "water.") Balanced on her head was a large tin can which seemed much too heavy for her fragile body. As she approached she kept up her ceaseless chant of "Kola—kola!" while at every syllable she clapped her hands together. When she caught sight of me she fell silent, watching in wide-eyed astonishment as I rode past.

Down another street came a second little girl, this time

with a Standard Oil tin on her head, and she shouted with all her might: "Ga-a-a-a-ssssss." By the time the last sibilant "s" had died away, she had recovered enough breath for her next announcement. The tin contained gasoline for the incandescent lamps which are used in nearly every native hut. Next came a lad pushing a wheelbarrow loaded with a barrel of ice. Port-au-Prince is very proud of her refrigerating plant!

A train, hauled by an antique locomotive, rattled along the street, the pedestrians leaping to right and left as it puffed through their midst. Out of the funnel sprayed a thick rain of sparks and glowing chips of wood. Children and grown-ups alike rushed forward to collect these splinters as spills for their pipes.

Beside me trotted a man carrying a coffin on his head and a little farther on was another man with a mahogany wardrobe balanced in a like manner.

From the market place came a terrific hubbub. I had been told that about ten thousand people gathered there every week to sell their goods to one another. My own eyes convinced me that that number was most certainly a conservative estimate. The vast square before the cathedral was packed with a countless multitude, all of whom contributed to the deafening noise composed of monologues, dialogues, chafferings, beggings, curses, and wild outbursts of rage. The goods causing all this excitement were laughably small in quantity and could scarcely have brought in very large profits.

Here is the inventory of a typical market stall.

Two bars of soap; a little heap of castor beans for lighting purposes; a broom, a leather strap, purses and cords of palm fiber, black tobacco, an umbrella, a heap of rusty nails, two empty bottles, matches tied with thread into bundles of twos and threes; a few pocket mirrors, some safety pins, and a battered spur completed the stock. Each transaction, no matter how small, commenced with a loud and lengthy argument, and ended, more often than not, in a fight.

A new marvel of commercial ingenuity was practiced by an old woman whom, out of curiosity, I followed right through the market. First, after some skillful bargaining, she bought a pumpkin for twenty cobs (about twopence), then she hawked the self-same vegetable through the crowd until she found a prospective purchaser. After an intricate and still more exciting debate, the pumpkin, now rather the worse for wear, was sold again for twenty cobs. Whereupon the old woman immediately departed with her money and, after more chattering, bought another pumpkin for twenty cobs. So she went round the whole day long, seeming to lay more value upon the volume of business transacted than upon the profits gained.

I pursued my way through the Rue de Liberté. A gang of convicts passed me carrying buckets of drinking water back to the prison. They wore uniforms like white bathing dresses encircled with red horizontal stripes. Behind them marched a soldier with rifle at the slope, muzzle in his hand and butt sticking into the air. His sole duty was to make sure that no more convicts returned into the prison than went out! Since the prison provides two large meals a day and a sheltered sleeping place it is a coveted sanctuary for paupers who have not even a roof over their heads. The government introduced prison uniform purely as a protection against idlers who liked to eat and sleep at the expense of the treasury. Such is Haiti!

I dismounted in front of the offices of the Caribbean Trading Company as I wanted to visit Assmusen, one of the directors who was a friend of mine. My card was taken in by a half-caste clerk and a few moments later I entered Assmusen's room. He was obviously in a raging temper although he did his best to conceal it before me. At last he could contain himself no longer and he poured out the whole sad story. It appeared that his Hamburg house had sent him a consignment of shoes which he was quite unable to dispose of. "These *gottverfluchten* niggers would rather become Christians than stuff their flat feet into shoes," he stormed, and he swore he would ship the whole load of "bloody muck" back to Hamburg by the first boat.

At that moment another business man came in, a kindred spirit in distress. He had just received a shipload of religious pictures printed in such modest, washy colors that they held no appeal for the sensation-loving native of Haiti. "Here in the tropics the saints have got to be printed good and bright before a nigger will even consider buying one. The only decent seller in this Voodoo pigsty is a dazzling, bloody Sacred Heart, pierced with thorns." So spoke the disillusioned salesman!

Assmusen had nothing more to say. He brought out a bottle of gin from behind his desk and began to drown his sorrows in silent drinking. It soon became noisy when his companion joined in, so I left the tippling pair after offering them my sincere condolences.

Outside the house I looked round—"Rosie" was gone! Then I saw her, in front of the post-office at the bottom of the hill; she had just snapped at the pink shirt of a ponderous gentleman (probably an official) who had come out of the post-office, and she had dragged the hinder portion of that beautiful garment out of his trousers. The wretched man forgot his dignity and scampered for the shelter of the nearest house to restore his clothing to a state of decency and to get away from the ribald laughter of the onlookers.

Among the women who were passing along the street, I noticed a great number who were wearing a curious addition to their costume. The customary white skirt had a patch of colored cloth, red, or blue, or red and blue, sewn on to the front like a sporran. These were the outward signs of the penances which the Papaloi had ordained as atonement for some transgression.

The actual penance was an exceedingly painful form of "mortification of the flesh." Below their usual clothing the sinners, women and girls, wore another garment, a "punishment dress." This consisted of a shirt, woven out of the thorny fibres of a certain palm and worn next to the skin so that every movement of the wearer caused a million tiny thorns to pierce and lacerate the flesh.

In an open space amongst the native huts stood an ornate bronze fountain. It was obviously a relic of the prosperous colonial era when it had played its fine spray in the gardens of some rich nobleman. Now it was very much out of place and only a disconsolate dribble of water issued from the dolphins' mouths. Round the fountain were gathered a group of women washing themselves. Their ablutions were simple in the extreme and not very hygienic. They caught the water in their cupped hands and poured it into their mouths. The resulting mixture was spat out into their hands again and then rubbed vigorously over their faces. The index finger of the right hand served as a toothbrush.

I rode onwards to the Champ de Mars.

Far off I espied the comic figure of Richard Messina. I had met him on my first ride through the town, a barefooted, gray-haired negro, wearing white concertina trousers, a shiny old frock coat, and a battered sun helmet perched on the back of his head; all insignia of his great respectability.

He greeted me as an old friend and addressed me in precise English: "Good-morning, mister, give me five cents." He took his tribute gracefully, waved his hand, and vanished into the crowd.

A garrulous bystander told me this old fellow's history. Once, a long time ago, he had been a respectable and respected lawyer and had even stood as candidate for the Presidency. For several years he had been the right-hand man of President Guillaume Sam, and as Master of Ceremonies he had had control of all visitors, his chief duty being to decide who was and who was *not* a fit person to meet the President. At last his vigilance failed. Sam was assassinated in 1915 by his dissatisfied subjects and Messina himself had to face a firing squad. Fortunately for him a reprieve arrived at the last moment, but the terrible shock he had received changed him from virtual dictator into a village idiot. . . .

Turning the corner by the "Café Eldorado," I found myself in the Champ de Mars, the chief square in Port-au-Prince. I passed a beautiful bronze statue representing a youth playing on a lyre, at the foot of which a market woman had tethered her mule. Opposite the boy there stood, on a disproportionately large stone base, the statue of Dessalines, national hero of Haiti, who was shown brandishing a saber. The sculptor had given Dessalines a peculiarly Caucasian cast of countenance, which was not surprising as the statue is said to represent, not Dessalines, but the champion of some South American state.

Fable has it that the state which originally commissioned the sculpture had a revolution and consequently their hero was forgotten before the work of art was finished. The new government quite naturally refused the statue, and the needy artist sold it (at the best price he could get) to the then President of Haiti, which wily man "discovered" it as an original of Dessalines and sold it (of course for a large profit) to the state.

In the middle of the Champ de Mars stands the White House, the President's palace. Its perfect architecture and lavishly beautiful decorations stand out in strange contrast to the poverty of the rest of the land. High, strong, wrought-iron railings run along the front of the building, not only for ornament but also to enclose the barracks of the U. S. Marines, which lie directly behind it. A Haitian President needs military protection more often than is pleasant or healthy for him!

For the same reason the square in front is kept clear of any vegetation, so that would-be assassins shall find no cover near the palace. Also, since the President's home is nearly always the center of a revolution, its construction resembles a fort more than a house. Twice in the course of the last hundred years the palace has flown into the air because the President insisted on keeping gunpowder stored in the cellars.

Haiti has experienced more political upheavals than any other country in the world. Its coat of arms, perhaps as a result of this, is martial in the extreme; in the middle, a palm tree with a sans-culotte cap perched on the top, on either side flags and cannons and between them a drum and a pyramid of cannon balls.

During my rides through Port-au-Prince and the neighborhood I often came across these massive great bronze cannons lying about. One was in the deserted Fort Francis, half buried in the sand; and there were some more in the middle of the town next door to the cathedral, where several breechless barrels lay across the pavement. They had probably lain there for decades, but with true tropical indolence the natives had always preferred to walk round them rather than to go to the trouble of moving them from where the revolutionaries had thrown them down. . . .

A piano was being transported across the cathedral square. By wagon? What!—in Haiti! Ten negroes stood round it pulling, pushing, lifting, and straining with as much unanimity as a coalition government. One section of the "removers" pushed forwards with fierce shouts of encouragement; the remainder pushed with equal ferocity in the opposite direction. They all heaved till the sweat poured down their backs. Then they paused for a breather and shouted at one another, arguing wildly across the top of the instrument. Eventually they seemed to have arrived at some decision, for the same performance started anew, only this time the first group pushed backwards while the others strained forwards. The wretched piano creaked and groaned in every joint and the lid flew open several times revealing a row of grinning ivory teeth. After I had watched the entertainment for some time, I moved on. Not so the piano. It probably stands on the same spot to this very day.

A little further along the road a new house was being erected in a more systematic fashion. A continuous line of negroes passed from the brickyard to the building site, each carrying one solitary brick on his head. With pathetically weary steps each industrious workman walked to the wall, cemented his contribution into place, and strolled just as slowly back to the yard to fetch a fresh supply. The foreman himself always accompanied one or other of the men and from the movements of his hands I could see that he had a good fund of humorous stories.

The incessant begging in Port-au-Prince was almost intolerable. If I pulled my horse up for one second to get a better view of some street scene, I was instantaneously surrounded by a troupe of beggars of all ages, holding out their filthy paws and shouting: "Mister, gimmi five cents!"

Once for a joke I gave an importunate child some money. His mother promptly asked me if I would care to buy her boy outright. Twenty-five dollars was the bargain price. Following the offer she lifted the dirty, kicking child into the air and made as though to place him in my lap.

I dug my spurs into "Rosie" just in time.

It was nearly noon.

From a clear blue sky the merciless equatorial sun blazed vertically overhead. It was odd how one stood on one's own shadow. The sea, an unruffled sheet of quicksilver, sent tired little ripples over the baking sand. A sailing boat hung motionless on the horizon. Cocoanut palms, twisted and bent by the wind into snake-like contortions, nodded their heads together and whispered secrets. The rays of the sun struck golden highlights off the glossy skins of the basking natives—on a day like this not even a negro could be black. It was unbearably and wonderfully hot.

The sea, an unruffled sheet of quicksilver, sent tired little ripples over the baking sand

The low, yellow houses on the Rue de Quai shimmered in the hot air like reflections in moving water. *Dolce far niente* held undisputed sway over the whole Antilles, changing each building, house, and hut into an enchanted palace. Under the shady patios of the residences the mistress dozed in her hammock. In the cool, dark bedrooms of the houses all were asleep. Even in the mud huts of the native quarter the whole family lay on a mat and snored. Amongst the dim palm groves I saw natives, standing, sitting, lying on cotton bales or on coffee sacks, all asleep—just as if Morpheus himself had walked through the streets, bewitching everyone with his magic wand. . . .

With a rattle and a bang all the office doors closed. The employees were free till four o'clock. Some went home; the majority of them forgathered in a low harbour "dive," whither I was also leading "Rosie."

From inside the cool, dark bar came the loud buzz of conversation. A motley cosmopolitan crowd was gathered round the rough wooden tables, talking and drinking. In one corner sat three clerks from a German export firm playing skat. Next to them was a party of American Marines. They drank whisky and spat often and accurately into the metal spittoon in the middle of the room. In a dark alcove sat some black Haitians, heads together, whispering. They were planning a coup d'état. Broken-down Europeans and beachcombers sat down beside each newcomer and begged for money or a drink. In the back room were gathered the sailors and officers of ships anchored in the harbor.

Another customer entered the bar behind me, his steps going flip-flap across the room. *Could it be true?* It was—my good old friend Perez. Captain José Perez, master of the *Santa Rita.* There was a joyful reunion and a great deal of embracing—but I adroitly avoided the rum-laden kiss that he tried to plant on my cheek. Soon I was seated amongst the tarry sailors in the back room, gossiping and drinking with my nautical friends.

I learned that the ship, which had coasted right round Santo Domingo, had only that morning cast anchor in Port-au-Prince harbor, where it was now loading logwood to be ready to sail again the same evening. On this next voyage the *Santa Rita* was bound for the Panama Canal, Ecuador, Peru, and down the west coast of South America. Wouldn't I go with them? This time, no—I unfortunately had to refuse, because I was due back in New York by a certain date. But another time . . . ?

Perez was disappointed. Still—he put his arm round my shoulders and whispered a weighty secret into my ear. Since our last meeting he had been practising drawing!! He would now like to show me his skill. I accordingly lent him one of my colored pencils and he proceeded to draw. . . . It was a sailing ship, in the portrayal of which he paid considerably more attention to technical detail than to art. This was evidently not his *métier*, for he left the ship half finished and tried his hand at women. Naked, fat, erotic female figures, which he embellished with as much care and detail as he had given to the ship. His proficiency in this branch of art was so advanced that he could draw women from every possible viewpoint—and in perspective too! From the front, from the back, from above, from below and from each side as well. The manner in which he drew his many-sided Venus was distinctly amusing. He began with an outline of broad, swinging hips; on top of them he set a full, round stomach, and above that a pair of voluminous breasts. . . . The remaining portions he sketched in with downright carelessness. They did not seem to interest him!

By general request I did a composite caricature of the party at our table, which was autographed by everyone, stuck in the frame of a whisky advertisement and hung on the wall. Then the hoarse voices of the seamen started a chanty chorus, other tables joined in, and soon the whole establishment was singing with us.

Pétionville.

Sometimes I left Jensen's villa just before daybreak and on those occasions I rode *up* the Rue Lalue. At such an early hour the road was completely empty except, perhaps, for two or three women carrying their goods to market. Once I met a solitary negro reeling home from an all-night "Bamboche." (The "Bamboche" is an open-air dance, usually held on Saturday evenings, which starts fairly respectably but which is apt to become, with the help of alcohol, extremely "free" and unrestrained.) This reveler talked loudly, first to himself and then to his partner (who was invisible); he gesticulated with his arms, turned sentimentally to his phantom girl-friend, and embraced her ecstatically, recalling memories of last night's amorous adventures.

As I trotted along the road which wound in snake-like bends up into the mountains, the sun shone out, lighting up the distant summits in a golden glow. In front of me and high above me towered the precipitous dark walls of Morne Hôpital and Morne Diable, while far away in the hazy distance stretched a long black shadow—the Cordillera, backbone of Santo Domingo. Gray clouds of morning mist rolled up the rocky slopes below me. Behind lay Port-au-Prince and the infinite blue sea. . . .

The clatter of "Rosie's" hoofs echoed hollowly through the streets of Pétionville. Nobody was awake to greet me. The broad square lay deserted. In the middle of it stood the compulsory "La Patrie," a royal palm tree with a daïs built round it. Behind the square a narrow jungle path led through a garden of indescribable beauty. I climbed the path until it wound out of sight of the town. Reality seemed far behind.

Wild orange trees grew in profusion all around me. Their branches bent under the weight of golden fruit, and as I passed three ripe oranges broke from their parent twig and rolled at my feet, a breakfast gift. Down below, in a deep valley, thousands of banana trees fluttered their broad leaves in the wind, looking for all the world like an emerald brook flowing between dark green forest walls. High above me, a black shadow against the azure sky, hovered a great bird of prey, his mighty wings beating powerfully—a condor from the gorges of the Cordillera.

Giant lizards at play ran up and down the sloping tree trunks. Their green color rendered them almost indistinguishable from the surrounding foliage except when they moved. As soon as they darted from sunlight into shadow their coloring changed to dark brown to match the bark of the trees. I sat down to rest under a wide sweeping tree that seemed hung with violins. It was actually a West Indian violin tree, so named from the curious shape of its leaves. Round about me soared the giant coffee trees, already hundreds of years old but still bearing heavy clusters of fruit.

I climbed up a gnarled fig tree whose lowest branches almost swept the ground. From the topmost bough I had a wonderful view of the bluest of all blue bays in the West Indies; a panorama which excelled even the famous vistas over the bays of Algiers and Naples. In front of me lay the Caribbean Sea, an endless crystal sheet of aquamarine broken only by the purple shadow of Gonave Island. A ship's siren screamed through the still air with painful intensity. A cargo boat cast off from its moorings and smoothly cleft through the blue waters until it vanished, a tiny speck, over the horizon.

At the foot of the tree a streamlet chattered by. I climbed down and followed its course until the murmuring waters broadened into a weir. Peering between the surrounding foliage I saw the naked figure of a young negress who stood motionless as a statue, knee-deep in the water with her arms crossed above her head. Through the palm leaves the hot sunlight played over her smooth body, burnishing the skin till it shone like fine black ebony. My presence in no way disturbed the dark beauty, for with a charming smile she said, "Bon jour, monsieur," and continued with her morning toilet.

Cap Haitien.

A stately palace once stood in the Place d'Armes, the main square of Cap Haitien. Here on the balcony surrounded by his staff, King Christophe took the salute of his troops; or in the reception hall he graciously received the homage of foreign emissaries. When his black majesty marched in formal procession to the church, no white man dared show his face among the kneeling crowds. . . . The Place d'Armes has known turbulent times. It was here that Dessalines organized the massacre of the white population. Here too, a few years later, the son and heir of King Christophe was executed.

Cap Haitien has forgotten.

Revolutions and an earthquake or two have destroyed the palace. On its site a cinema stands today. The entrance hall becomes at evening a fashionable rendezvous for the young negresses who all day long walk about in a simple shift and at night appear wearing white dresses, stockings, and high-heeled shoes, their faces powdered to a pale violet shade and their lips painted carmine. Black dandies in straw hats stroll self-consciously up and down outside until each one has succeeded in securing for himself a willing "partner" to escort into the movies. One night I joined the pleasure-seeking throng and found myself in a dark, ill-ventilated room where all the audience were talking at the top of their voices and gesticulating wildly.

A momentary hush fell as a yellowed picture flashed onto the screen. A minute later the conversations were in full spate again. It made no difference to the entertainment, for we were shown some silent films of extremely ancient vintage. It seemed to me that all the old pictures of the Max Linder-John Bunny era had found a final resting place in Haiti, and it was impossible to help noticing their great age because wherever a section of the original film was missing a bit of another film was inserted which never by any chance had the faintest resemblance to the first body onto which it had been

I saw the naked figure of a young negress

CARCASS

grafted! After a time the old film reappeared again and the story resumed its interrupted course.

But what did the audience care for the phantoms on the tarnished silver screen. They were far too deeply engaged with their partners to notice anything else.

Once when a particularly scratched reel was running through the machine, a young negress beside me awoke from her trance and murmured to her beau: "What a pity that the rain comes into the parlor and makes the beautiful white lady so wet!"

Petit Anse.

The bay was deserted, the shore empty. Only a few mussels and strands of seaweed were washed by the tide. I walked round the semicircular beach in which silvery sand alternated with broad strips of brown swampy mud, and as I walked I stumbled over a cannon buried in the sand. I did not pause to examine the barrel as I usually would have done. but hurried on towards my destination. At last I reached a crumbling jetty against which no ship had lain for years. Nevertheless, this useless stone pier marked the spot where, centuries ago, the most famous ship in history ran aground.

On Christmas Eve of the year 1492 the *Santa Maria*, Columbus's flagship, splintered on a coral reef during a typhoon. The crew and their captain all got safely ashore. With the help of the inhabitants of the island and their king, Guacanagaric, the shipwrecked sailors rebuilt their vessel.

There, on a little knoll to my right, the Genoese adventurer had erected the first building of the white men in the New World, Fort "La Natividad." When Columbus returned the following year, the fort and its garrison of forty-eight men had completely vanished. Throughout my stay in Haiti nothing aroused more memories of the adventurous past than the sight of that bare little hill. Today the scene was different from that memorable Christmas Eve. A few miserable huts leant drunkenly against the wind-blown palms. In front of one of them a bronze cannon stuck vertically out of the ground with the "N" of Napoleon proudly engraved on its barrel. . . .

Many years ago some fishermen trawling in the bay had hauled up the anchor of the *Santa Maria* in their nets. During the World's Fair at Chicago in 1893 this anchor had been one of the chief exhibits, and now it lies in the Gendarmerie at Port-au-Prince. When Lindbergh opened the Antilles air route in 1928, the grateful Haitians presented him with a silver letter-weight in which was embedded a tiny piece of rusted iron—from the anchor of the *Santa Maria*.

Grande Rivière.

The weekly train that wandered into the hinterland of Haiti stood in the station at Cap Haitien ready to depart. A locomotive whose appearance was strangely reminiscent of Stephenson's museum piece was belching out clouds of smoke and ashes in its impatience to be off. Inscribed in ornate gold lettering on its boiler front was the sonorous title:

"*Compagnie Nationale des Chemins de Fer d'Haiti*"

A description that was duplicated in miniature on every compartment door. Besides the engine the train was composed of a tender full of wood, a first-class carriage that looked about as comfortable as a tramcar, and two other carriages, more like cattle trucks than anything else, which were provided for the less prosperous travelers.

In spite of the early hour, for it was just after six o'clock, half Cap Haitien had turned up to give the train a rousing send-off. A few of those present were travelers, others were friends and relations saying a last farewell, but the great majority of the crowd were sightseers who had simply come to gaze and gossip. Hawkers were selling sweetmeats of various kinds and an old negress did a brisk trade in beer which she dispensed from a large bottle. For five cobs she poured a few precious drops of liquid into the dirty, outstretched hands of the purchaser who lapped up the beer, frugally licking his palms into a state of unnatural cleanliness.

At the last minute Monsieur le Conducteur appeared on the scene, panting into the station on a rusty iron bicycle. With one accord the passengers stormed the carriages. Market baskets filled with raucously protesting hens were pushed beneath the seats; men, women, and children wedged themselves on top. The last door had scarcely slammed, when the "toot" of a tin trumpet pierced the hubbub, the signal for departure.

Nothing happened.

The conductor ran wildly up and down the train. . . . What was wrong? Ah—the engine driver had been forgotten! A feverish search; he was found! He strolled out of a near-by hut and climbed nonchalantly onto the foot plate. After a moment's breathless expectancy the engine gave a loud snort and the train jerked back a foot; then—wonder of wonders—the whole rackety contraption steamed slowly forwards.

We had started.

Negroes were still jumping on and off the footboard. An old woman ran along the train and thrust a hen crate through the window. Then we rattled across a bridge and the last of our pursuers was left behind. The railway was single track, narrow gauge, and lay for the first mile or two alongside the Santo Domingo road. Then it branched off and plunged into the jungle.

A negro in Holy Orders pushed his way through the passengers singing Latin psalms interspersed with an occasional "Benedicat vos omnipotens Deus" whenever someone put a coin into his collection box. Many of the travelers were on a pilgrimage to Bahón and the money that went into Père Codada's box was destined to finance the renovation of the church there.

The train halted in the middle of the jungle where a station was indicated by a post with a derelict lantern wired to the top. Nobody got out here but dozens of fresh passengers performed the miracle of accommodating themselves in carriages already crammed to their painful capacity. The newcomers were accompanied by a weird assortment of "luggage" which naturally had to come aboard too. One negro carried a struggling goat slung round his neck. Others brought huge bundles of dyewoods with them, and as none of the passengers wanted such a weight dumped on their toes, they all drew their feet back under the seat when such a bundle was thrown in through the door. Half-a-dozen casks of rum were accorded a similar reception, but they at least provided some much-needed seating accommodation. A basket of fighting cocks completed our discomfort!

While all this was happening the conductor had seized the opportunity of visiting a friend whose hut lay somewhere in the neighboring jungle. It was his custom every week to have his half hour's or even hour's gossip with this particular friend, returning from it happy and refreshed.

At length we started off again; but just as the train was getting under way a young negro squeezed into my compartment and settled himself with as much comfort as possible on a rum barrel, as if preparing for a long, long journey. He lay back against the nearest pair of knees, closed his eyes, and grinned all over his face. For him this crawling train meant the rapturous means of escape into the wide and wonderful world beyond. So I thought. But I was wrong; for directly the train began to gather speed the young traveler waved farewell and sprang out into the bush.

The track ran for a little way alongside a lagoon. Huge bunches of bananas shone golden-yellow against the rich background of green leaves. Along the further shore were bamboo huts standing on stakes above the water. A child, not more than three years old, paddled about in a canoe, while his parents dozed tranquilly in the darkness of their hut undisturbed even by the rattle of the train. The scene vanished as we plunged into the jungle again. . . .

At last we reached the terminus, another rusty lantern, where I stretched my cramped legs and climbed out of the carriage.

Bahón.

I rested awhile in the shady patio of Café San Juanita. The noonday sun drew up heavy waves of air, making the limewashed houses across the square shimmer in the heat. The white walls made one's eyes ache with the intensity of their glare. It was impossible to look at them for long. In front of the café the black youths of Bahón ran and jumped and danced, seemingly unaware of the terrific heat. Today was a red-letter day, for the weekly train had brought ice from Cap

Haitien, the first consignment for several months. The children played with little chips of it. Many of them had never seen ice before and they quarreled amongst themselves as to whether these funny "stones" that melted so quickly were really hot or cold.

Next to me sat Major MacPhearson of the American garrison and he told me strange stories of the Cacos rebellion. . . . Bahón lay in the area which had been the center of the fighting.

The Cacos are as closely woven into the history of Haiti as Voodoo or King Christophe. Sixty years ago, when the patriots of the Republic rebelled against President Salnave, they were driven back after fierce fighting into the interior of the island, and, since their retreat to the sea was cut off, they settled down to live in the bush. From this impregnable position they carried on a guerilla warfare and made marauding sorties into the surrounding country. After a while the original patriotic fervor of their cause died away and they recruited an enormous number of unscrupulous rascals to swell their band which now existed for solely criminal purposes. They called themselves Cacos (*parrots*) and their opponents (now consisting of all law-abiding people), whom they were trying to exterminate, Caterpillars.

Again and again the largest towns in the island were raided by these "patriotic" robbers, who vanished as mysteriously as they came, usually carrying off much valuable booty. Should a President overstep the bounds of his authority or a new leader raise the flag of revolt the Cacos were at hand to execute and avenge. They had everything to gain and nothing to lose. They sallied out of their mountain fastness, putting everything that came in their path to flame or the sword. Deeds of bestial cruelty were committed by them,

Bamboo huts standing on stakes above the water

but since they were strong adherents of Voodoo they had friends and connections in every part of the country and consequently feared no retribution. Thus the Cacos impoverished the whole of Haiti. Cattle disappeared almost completely from the land, all devoured by the hungry raiders. There was no peace to be had till the American Marines wiped the band off the face of the earth.

When the Marines arrived, an educated negro, one Charlemagne Massena Peralte, collected a large number of the Cacos round him in order to rid Haiti of the "interfering foreigners." A great part of the population hailed him as the champion of his country and rallied to him with enthusiasm. This troop of freebooters used to sweep down on defenceless villages, commandeer all the food, and press the men into the service of Charlemagne's "army." Haiti became one huge nest of bandits.

Charlemagne, on whose head a high price was set, knew how to hide himself safely and all efforts at finding him were in vain until one day a non-commissioned officer, by name Herman H. Hanneken, volunteered single-handed to track the chief to his headquarters, in a corner of the mountains between Bahón and Grande Rivière, and there to destroy him.

Even then, for a long time, every effort was futile. Charlemagne was no fool; he smelt a rat and avoided every trap however skillfully laid. The situation was now beginning to assume an alarmingly critical aspect. Affairs were desperate and the Cacos became ever more daring, for, in the eyes of his followers, Charlemagne's continued freedom was attributable directly to his supernatural powers.

However, Hanneken was a man of quick decision and indomitable determination. He and an officer, Lieutenant

Button, decided to make a surprise attack. The two of them blacked their bodies and clothed themselves in smelly rags so that they might be taken for members of the Cacos. Then they started out at dead of night for the enemy headquarters —with the component parts of a portable machine gun hidden under their tattered clothing. Traveling by night and hiding by day, they reached the chieftain's stronghold, and although there were six concentric circles of scouts guarding Charlemagne's camp, the Americans, owing to their intimate knowledge of Creole, got past each one unsuspected. The machine gun barked out its deadly message. . . .

With the death of Charlemagne the Cacos menace was broken. Hanneken was promoted out of the ranks, and since then he has again distinguished himself. In 1930 he captured the dreaded rebel leader, Jiron, in the forests of Nicaragua.

Anse Rouge.

Pierre Lepreux was the chemist in Anse Rouge.

In his little shop he practised cures of many sorts, most of them unknown to his European brethren. He had to keep a large and weird assortment of medicaments, for natives demand many curious things which according to their beliefs have great healing power. But that Monsieur Lepreux possessed an unusually wide range of pharmaceutic knowledge there was no denying. He used to go into the forest and collect personally hundreds of different roots and leaves with which to accommodate his exacting customers. Many of these therapeutic plants are not known, even by name, to the white man; only the negro realizes and values the medicinal powers which they possess.

One day I was exploring round the shop when a large wooden box labeled "*Animaux morts*" aroused my curiosity. I drew it out of the cupboard, raised the lid—and quickly shut it again. A dank, mouldy smell emanated from the box which was filled to the brim with little dried animals; mice, rats, moles, bats, and various birds.

"Fetishes," said Monsieur Lepreux laconically.

He saw my derisive smile and shook his head disapprovingly. "You come to me," he said, "to find out about native lore, and yet you would laugh scornfully if I told you about sorcery, and you would most certainly despise me if I admitted that I too believe in the healing power of those dead animals. Well, I do." He spoke defiantly now. "You are a white man which means that you associate the word 'magic' only with conjuring and such-like hocus-pocus. With us negroes things are otherwise, and—whether you believe them or not—they lie much deeper.

"We live here, in a tropical forest, among men whose forefathers came from Africa, men who have transplanted their thousand-year-old cults of magic to the New World. In an unbroken line the medicine men have received their sacred inheritance from their fathers; even here, in Haiti, their new home. Magic is the one great reality of jungle life; since unremembered time it has been fostered and developed. It teaches the black man how he must live, and how he can protect himself against the terrible dangers that always surround him.

"What is there so ridiculous about fetishes and amulets? Since the beginning of the world man has created his own gods, distinguishing the god of light from the god of darkness and founding his beliefs on his appreciation of cause and effect. He experienced with terror and amazement the mighty disturbances which nature wrought upon his home—the earth; thunder and lightning, storms, eruptions, earthquakes. And realizing that such things cannot happen of themselves, he was afraid of his own insignificance, and he created his first god. More problems arose and new gods offered their solution; for every problem a new god. A firm belief in the reality of your god is half the answer to your prayer.

"Finally, haven't you Christians used the same idea; only a European version of it? Laugh at the negroes! You understand them as little as they understand you. The black race is far closer to the earth than the white, and for that reason they are happier than all the white men put together. A negro believes without asking why; he submits to nature.

"Perhaps you might like to make an expedition with me this afternoon which I hope may prove to you better than all my arguments the intimate understanding between the negro and nature."

That afternoon I rode out of Anse Rouge beside Lepreux. Our way led past wide sugar and tobacco fields, but not a soul was stirring. Every place was deserted in the mid-day heat. Soon we had left the town behind and as we forded a brook I was surprised to see a solitary negress wading across with her skirts held high above the water. I wondered where she could be going, so far from any habitation. Half a mile further on we turned into the forest and Lepreux signaled me to dismount. We led the horses into a little thicket so that they would be concealed from any thieving eyes and tied them to a tree. Then we continued on foot, breaking our way

In the doorway appeared a young negress

through the undergrowth until we struck a narrow jungle path which after a few minutes opened into a clearing. In the middle of the clearing was a hut, and in front of the hut a tall stake had been driven into the ground and a horse's skull hung on the top. We had arrived at the "Houmfort," the Voodoo prayer-house.

We were still under the cover of the trees, and Lepreux whispered to me to stay where I was till he returned. It would be most unfortunate for both of us if I were to be caught in the sacred place by any of the worshipers. With this warning he crept across to the hut and peered cautiously in through one of the windows; then he straightened up and beckoned me. The coast was clear, and I followed him into the building.

We found ourselves in a medium-sized room, with a table in the middle and empty boxes ranged round the walls to serve as chairs. On the table stood a few dusty cups and plates. To the left of the door hung the primitively carved head of an animal with long, pointed ears, possibly representing a hare. But the chief exhibit of the "Houmfort" was a life-sized human statue, cut out of wood and extremely ill-proportioned. This effigy, obviously representing a male figure, had an oval head, slit eyes, and a nose like a gherkin. Out of its half-opened mouth a long tongue hung down over its chin. The tall, cylindrical body was decorated with ornamental carving and out of the lower end projected a piece of wood about the size and shape of a large cudgel. Lepreux drew me aside into the next room which was pitch dark and full of wooden billets, probably used as stools at times of great festivity, and here we sat and waited for what might happen.

The time passed slowly, but after half an hour we heard

footsteps approaching across the clearing. Lepreux pressed my hand as a sign that I must on no account betray my presence by the slightest sound or movement. . . .

In the doorway appeared a young negress with a basket balanced on her head. She placed the basket on the floor and took out of it fruit, food, and some bottles of palm wine, all of which she laid carefully on the table. I recognized her now as the woman whom we had overtaken at the ford.

When the basket was empty, she peeped out of the door to make sure no one was coming, and then she took a bottle of wine in each hand and poured the contents over various parts of the fetish, intoning the while some ritual chant in a mixture of Creole and African dialects. Her voice ranged from an astonishingly deep contralto to a high falsetto. After this, and still singing, she placed the food and fruit on the floor at the feet of the idol and lit some candles. When everything was arranged to her satisfaction she knelt down and carried on an animated conversation with the wooden figure, pointing first at its mouth and then at the outspread offerings. A torrent of words poured from the girl with fearful intensity. She seemed to be overwhelming her god with reproaches and accusations, which he, seeing he was only made of wood, was in no position to refute. Her prayers became more and more voluble until, in a moment of ecstasy, she sprang astride the knees of the carved monster, and, continuing to upbraid him, alternately hammered on his unresponsive body and embraced the emblems of his fertility. When she had finished, she placed the empty basket on her head and, still gabbling to herself, vanished into the sunlight.

Lepreux offered me a cigarette which I gratefully accepted and we returned to our horses.

Plaine de Gonaïves.

If anyone were to ask me which is the hottest place on earth, I would unhesitatingly reply: "Gonaïves."

The town lies in the middle of a dazzling white sand waste which becomes so hot under the baking rays of the sun that it blisters the soles of the feet, and the unfortunate traveler who has to pass that way might well imagine that he, like an Indian fakir, was walking over red-hot coals. During my short stay there I spent my whole time and energy cursing the infernal heat. It infuriated me; the more so as I seemed to be the only person there who noticed the soaring thermometer. Certainly the negroes did not care. I suppose it was because the sun's rays reflected harmlessly off their oily skins.

The contrasts of climate in Haiti are almost unbelievable to one who has never experienced them. In the north of the island along Massacre River I had endured a tropical cloudburst when solid walls of water fell for days on end. But here, in the south of the same island, the country between Gonaïves and St. Marc had not felt a drop of rain for several months. Day after day the tropical sun, directly overhead, blazed down on the parched and crumbling earth, and all around lay the undulating white sand like the floor of an immense furnace.

I wore as little as possible; a white duck suiting that a tailor in Cap Haitien had made for me, and a new topee which replaced the old one ruined on my expedition to Dajabon. But even this bare minimum of clothing was well nigh unbearable in the heat. I wished that I was only a fleshless skeleton or at least covered with a thick, cool black skin!

As soon as was possible I pushed on to my next destination. By a stroke of luck I managed to charter a car in Gonaïves. It would have been as quick to walk! Every few yards we had to stop to allow the engine to cool off. After the first five minutes the red needle of the radiator thermometer had passed the danger mark and could go no further without bursting. How the machinery ran at all without melting was a miracle.

It was wonderful how nature had provided something in the way of vegetation even for this arid land. Giant cacti grew in the strangest shapes and forms to a height of thirty or forty feet and bore flowers of pink, yellow, and violet hues. Animals who stray into the desert break the stems of these remarkable plants with their hooves and drink the juicy sap which always flows in abundance no matter how long the drought has already lasted.

On our journey through this wilderness we passed several solitary graves whose tombstones were all made in the shape of miniature churches. One of the strangest of these graves was the tomb of a Mamoloi; a futuristic affair with the coffin visible through the little doorway. The decorations were of particular interest, being a circle containing the symbol of

Damballa the snake-god, surmounted by a cross. Many of the tombstones were badly mutilated by the driving sand. Here and there a skull still covered with hair grinned out of the ground at us. Indeed the whole place was very like a charnel house, for all along the road lay the bleached bones of the unfortunate animals that had died of thirst or starvation.

On the horizon appeared the silhouette of St. Marc. We were nearly there. But just before we reached the town we met with one of nature's most curious phenomena: a sand-spout. At first it was quite small and circular, a little pillar of sand. Then it began rotating with ever-increasing speed, drawing more and more sand into its vortex, and growing enormously in size until it attained the height of a house. At the same time it began to move slowly forwards. On the edge of the road it stopped, as if waiting for us to pass.

We took a deep breath, shut our eyes—and accelerated. There was sand everywhere. We were smothered in it: eyes, ears, nose, all smarted and tickled. The car was quite white and on the floor was a layer of grit several inches deep.

So we passed the outlying huts of St. Marc.

St. Marc.

I was sitting outside the Café St. Rose beside Major Delehanty of the U. S. Marines. The Major was Irish. In front of him stood a glass of fizzy lemonade—it had stood there for the last half hour while we discussed wines, a subject in which the Major was obviously well versed. But at the moment he was not at his ease, for every now and again he frowned at his wrist-watch as if some unpleasant duty were awaiting him. By dint of questioning I elicited the fact that he also held a commission as captain in the Haitian gendarmerie, dividing his time equally between the Marines and the Black Republic.

This was plainly the cause of his disquietude, for, as the church clock struck twelve, the Major pushed the lemonade aside—his duties as Haitian officer had commenced. He ordered a whisky and soda. This seemed more to his taste, as evidenced by the rapidity with which he gulped it down and ordered another. One more, and then we had to go.

When we arrived at the barracks, we found a tremendous commotion going on. About a hundred black soldiers were falling in for health inspection. I was told that President Borno himself was expected to visit the parade. Ten minutes later a dusty Hudson car turned into the barracks square and pulled up before the troops. Two soldiers with Winchester rifles jumped from the car and opened the door. The President and his daughter stepped out. His Excellency President Louis Borno was a small, dapper man with gray hair and an intelligently shaped head. His skin was of that peculiar pale brown hue that indicates a mulatto origin.

I was formally introduced to him. There was a moment's silence while two piercing eyes behind a pair of pince-nez summed me up. Then he addressed me in perfect English.

While we stood there chatting, the national drink of rum and water was handed round, after which refreshment the President, insisting that I should accompany him, proceeded to inspect the troops.

Miragoâne.

The negro cemetery at Miragoâne resembled a tiny town by reason of the little whitewashed house, church, or tower which stood on each grave. Here and there were large mausoleum-like memorials with deep niches wherein mouldered the remains of thank-offerings. Baron Samedi, Lord of the Underworld, is wont to be troublesome if he finds empty niches!

The Haitians fill up their burial grounds without any idea of symmetry or order and the one at Miragoâne was no exception. The corpses were buried just where they could be fitted in, so close together at some places that it seemed as though the coffins must have been stood on end beside each other.

When a man dies a festive holiday is immediately declared for the whole neighborhood. The nearest relations give a banquet and the dead man is dressed in his best clothes and set on a chair at the head of the table so that he too may partake of the merry-making. After the guests have drunk their fill, the body is put into its coffin and carried to the cemetery. Behind the coffin walks "Papa Beaucoup," Voodoo priest and doctor combined, grasping in his right hand a large bottle of rum with which he periodically strengthens the pall-bearers and, of course, himself. The women in mourning clothes follow after, singing the customary obscene songs. At every cross-roads they pause, look anxiously round, and then run quickly over to the other side. Everybody knows that the devil lurks at cross-roads! In this fashion the procession staggers along to the graveyard. Everyone seems to be enjoying himself thoroughly. Even the corpse has some amusement, for the reeling and swaying of the rum-laden bearers often precipitates him from his loosely carpentered coffin onto the roadway. When this happens the body is lifted up again with much shouting and laughter and shoved back into the wooden box which is finally and without much ceremony dropped into a grave.

Aux Cayes.

The prosperity of Haiti flows in and out through the waterfront of Aux Cayes. Export and import, the two great pillars of international trade, dominate the docks, cranes, warehouses, and steamers in the harbor.

What a medley of cargoes lying on the quay! Barrels of oil from Boston, kegs of butter from Denmark, dried fish from Norway, hardware, chemicals, and medicaments from Germany. . . .

And outward bound; the home products of the towns,

fields, and jungles of Haiti. Casks of cotton oil and rum, bundles of sugar cane, bales of cotton, bunches of bananas, piles of tobacco leaves, cocoa, mahogany planks, dyewoods, and—above all—*coffee*. Miles of coffee, walls of sacks piled house-high, scenting the air with a delicious smell that drowns all others. Aux Cayes must be the sweetest smelling harbor on earth.

Coffee is the wealth of Haiti and it grows abundantly on the rich brown surface soil of the island. But it is a delicate plant. It will only flourish in a tropical climate and yet, at the same time, it must be in a cool, shady place. To this end, it is planted in long straight rows under spreading banana or mango trees. In spring the plantation looks like a beautifully laid out park, with charming walks between the verdant avenues of trees. And then, one sunny morning, every branch is smothered with flowers like apple blossom in May, garlands of white stretching from tree to tree in wonderful profusion. It is but a passing glory, for overnight the blossom vanishes and only the long green leaves are left to flutter in the wind.

Tropical downpours and sweltering heat force the berries which hang on their twigs like bright red cherries to early fruition. In every berry lie two coffee beans.

At harvest time nimble black fingers pluck the berries into large wicker baskets which are then piled into primitive ox carts. When all the carts are loaded the caravan starts off, lurching along the narrow jungle track on the way back to the trading post where the products of all outlying plantations are collected. Carts, row upon row, wait outside the building until each one's turn comes to unload. A chain of natives hand down the baskets and tip the sticky red berries into long wooden troughs while the boss stands by and counts the troughfuls that vanish into the silo. The driver of the caravan is given a receipt for the amount he has delivered and then, squatting on the foremost wagon, he drives off again into the jungle.

At this stage modern industry takes a hand in the destiny of the coffee beans. They are shelled, cleaned and dried in various machines, being delivered from the one to the other in a fast-flowing stream of water. Like magic the two chief parts of the beans are separated; on the one side the evil-smelling, rotten husks, and on the other, piles of wet golden beans. The latter are spread out in great heaps in the sun and from time to time they are shoveled over to make sure they shall all dry equally. It is a delicious sensation to plunge one's arm into the piles of coffee and let the beans trickle through the fingers.

The coffee, which by now has lost all traces of its husk, is taken into the adjacent "barracks" whence comes the loud and incessant chatter of hundreds of negresses. Each woman sits on her own pile of coffee, sorting the beans. In front of her are several broad baskets for the reception of various grades of beans and over the baskets her arms hover as expertly as though performing some cabalistic Voodoo ritual. The speed with which these women work is incredible; their movements are almost too rapid for the eye to follow. The workers are a happy crowd and everything goes merrily—that is, provided the weather is fine. But should the sky become overcast and dull, the sensitive spirits of the negresses drop. They sit in front of their sorting baskets sad and silent, and the work proceeds much slower than on sunny days. Peevish words fly to and fro; the quarreling gathers in volume until it not infrequently leads to hand-to-hand fights, at which point the boss comes in and restores order with a firm hand.

The coffee is now ready for export. It is sewn up in sacks and conveyed to the nearest port where it vanishes into the hold of a steamer and travels across to Europe.

Tea is served in Japan with the strictest ceremony, said to endow it with a specially delicious flavor.

In Haiti they also have their ancient customs. The natives roast the coffee until it is nearly black, then they grind it, and, by filtering hot water through the grounds, they obtain a thick aromatic coffee-essence. First thing in the morning, at six o'clock, the servant of the house brings in a tray loaded with a cup, a bowl of sugar, a jug of hot water, and a smaller jug of cold coffee-essence. The mixing then follows. Some of the essence is poured into the cup, the actual amount varying according to personal taste, and then the hot water is added until the brew is sufficiently diluted. The black "Donna" is quite indifferent as to whether her thus early awakened guest is in a fit state to receive her or not; she simply pulls up a chair, sits down, and exposes her white teeth in a broad grin as she watches the proceedings.

Such is the coffee ceremony in Haiti!

Jérémie.

Father Maurice de Cacqueray, member of the seminary, invited me to visit his library. It would, he assured me, be a visit well worth while to anyone who was at all interested in history and books. I gladly accepted and at the appointed time I found him standing beside the seminary gates, waiting to receive me. After a brief greeting he turned and led me up a flight of wooden steps. At the top a high door, lavishly ornamented with baroque carvings, opened before me. The priest himself withdrew discreetly.

I found myself in a spacious silent room dimly lighted by the sun which struggled in through the fast-closed lattice windows and traced a twisted pattern on the floor. All round the walls and up to the ceiling rose tiers of old-fashioned bookcases and in the middle of the room stood a large revolving globe. I made a rapid tour round the shelves, drawing out a book from here and there and dipping into its contents. Ancient geographical works bound in calf jostled against modern novels; all books which had traveled across the sea to find a final resting place in this silent room.

An ancient cupboard standing in one corner caught my eye. In the antique lock stuck a great hand-forged key. Overcome with curiosity I turned the key and pulled open the creaking door. The shelves inside were chock ablock with books, French and English, piled in wild confusion, where they had evidently been thrown in to make space on the bookshelves round the walls for newer and more important works. I tried to produce some order out of the chaos, taking the books out one by one and glancing through them before I laid them on the floor. By the time I had finished, the inside of the cupboard was as neat as could be, with rows of neatly ranged books, and I too had had my reward, for during my self-imposed task I discovered several volumes of more than passing interest.

There was a volume of local history by the English ambassador, Harvey, dated 1827; *Sketches of Hayti from the Expulsion of the French to the Death of Christophe.* Lying beneath it was Mackenzie's *Notes on Hayti*, a pamphlet published in 1830. Neither of these merited more than a cursory examination.

Here was something better. A fat octavo book with no title on the binding. I picked it up and glanced inside. The volume bore the imprint of the Royal Press of King Christophe at Sans Souci, and on the title page I read: *Almanach Royal d'Hayti, pour l'année 1818, Présenté au Roi par Buon.* An odor of mildew and venerable age rose from the yellowed leaves as I turned them over. The past was dead and gone, the régime was forgotten, but I could almost hear the rustling of satins and lace ruffles as I glanced down the lists of the noble aristocracy founded by King Christophe. They were all there, all that was left of that strange kingdom—the royal family, the princes, barons, knights, down to the smallest page, placed in the order of their precedence. What a strange time that must have been when the splendors of a negro king rivaled even the pristine glories of Versailles. Everything the same, only their skins were black. . . . Yes—*there* was a chapter on court etiquette; it seemed to have been strictly enforced in those days. Christophe had been successful in his ambitions. He had built up a court of incomparable grandeur—and his end was even more terrible than that of the unhappy Bourbons. . . .

Another book was called *Reflexions politiques par Monsieur le Baron de Vastey;* the author had been Christophe's secretary. There was also an ancient prayer-book in French and English, published for the especial use of the royal and national schools. One after another I took the books out. The cupboard was nearly empty now; only a few odd papers and pamphlets were left on the topmost shelf. I picked up an official-looking document printed on yellowing parchment. It bore the signature of the great Napoleon. It was a proclamation which the Emperor's brother-in-law, Le Clerc had brought on his ill-fated expedition to Haiti. There was a date at the top—"17. Brumaire in the Tenth Year of the French Republic"—and the manifesto ended with the warning: "I repeat once again, 'Obey Le Clerc; who fails in this is a traitor to his country, and the curse of the Republic will destroy him even as fire consumes the dry sugar-cane.' Signed: Bonaparte." And now it was relegated to the rubbish cupboard in order to make way for more modern books on philosophy and science. So much for the great!

There were still two heavy dusty tomes hidden away in one corner. No good! They were only obsolete treatises on theology; but sandwiched between them was something else, a little pamphlet bound in green paper which looked as though it might prove interesting. I drew it out and glanced at the title page. The wordy heading ran as follows: "*A Scientific Expedition to the West Indian Island of Haiti, financed by His Majesty the Emperor of Austria and Undertaken by Karl Ritter, Botanical Director of Hungary and Member of Several Learned Societies. Stuttgart 1824.* The author's foreword, a breathless sentence of sixteen lines, informed me that Herr Ritter "burned with the desire to extend his knowledge in the realms of Natural Science and to explore to the full the luxuriant tropical nature of Haiti." In order to further the success of this expedition the Viennese Society of Naturalists had presented the gallant leader with six chests full of Austrian minerals as a gift for King Christophe.

I read further.

Herr Ritter went on to describe the arduous twenty-six days' journey from Trieste to Cap Haitien. How jubilant they all were when the island hove in sight and they at last dropped anchor in front of Cap Haitien. And then the bitter blow fell. They were forbidden to land!

It was Christophe's command. Not even the six chests of minerals (there were some rare fossils as well) could soften the king's harsh attitude. But Herr Ritter was not the man to despair or to retreat at the first obstacle that arose. No! He knew that the king lived far inland and also that a vassal duke ruled over Cap Haitien. Very well, the duke was the man to approach. By devious and skillful means the little Austrian made friends with the Duke of Marmalade, Christophe's brother-in-law; and this was easier than might be imagined, for the duke was already contemplating revolt against his sovereign.

Ritter was allowed to land and was even given a house outside Cap Haitien. But that was the limit. Any further exploration was forbidden on pain of death, for Haiti was, as the duke pointed out, taboo for white men. In spite of this restriction Ritter found nature in abundance round the neighborhood of Cap Haitien, as was shown in his enthusiastic account of his discoveries. Moreover, he lived there up to the period of chaos that followed the tragic death of King Christophe.

Directly he heard that the king was dead, he set out in brave defiance of his late majesty's injunction for the interior of the island and he was actually the first white man to see Sans Souci after it had been plundered by the mob. I found his description of the ransacked palace extraordinarily interesting—it was probably the only eye-witness account still in existence—or, indeed, ever written. Continuing with his story, the courageous professor himself admitted that he was far too frightened to explore any further; he dared not push on to the Citadel of La Ferrière, much as he longed to see that terrible and forbidden fortress. He turned his back on the gutted palace and the howling mob and retreated to the coast. Then, heavily laden with the rich trophies of the tropics, Karl Ritter sailed for home.

By the time I had finished reading the pamphlet the sun was already low behind the palm trees and the twisted shadow of the window had crept across the floor and up the opposite shelves. I stacked the books back in the cupboard as tidily as possible, and then opened a protesting window to let the cool evening air into the room. Outside on the road little columns of red dust danced gayly in the last fading rays of the sun. I could see across to the mountains where dark shadows climbed inch by inch up their rocky flanks, shrouding them in sleep. Suddenly a soft vibration thrilled the air. It was coming from one of the distant gorges. It started gently and grew louder and louder, throbbing with ever greater intensity. It died away. And then it started again; the light boo-om-boo-om of a drum. What message did it carry to the quiet countryside around? The same message as a hundred years ago—as a hundred years hence. The message of a hungry god. . . .

Father Maurice accompanied me to the garden gate, and as we walked down the path I heard the subdued murmur of holy men, praying—to another God.

Coraïl.

The native boat rocked lightly on the smooth waters of the bay. A brilliant full moon threw its ghostly mantle of silver light over the nocturnal landscape, changing the world of the living to a world of phantoms, until it seemed that we were sailing over fairy waters through a soundless vacuum of imagination. Even the crowing of a sleepy cock left the peaceful silence undisturbed.

On shore was darkness; not a light—Coraïl slept.

Eugène, the fisherman, made fast the fiber sail and drew

out from under the seat a guitar. The soft twanging of its steel strings harmonized sweetly with the melody of an old Spanish song. The scene was perfect. A warm, mysterious, breathless, moonlit night, a rippling sea—and music; not the harsh jazz of the sophisticated city, but the liquid notes of a guitar; and the strong voice of a sailor instead of the emasculated twitterings of some sickly crooner. The boat drifted in space. . . .

Suddenly a wind sprang up and drove us away from land. The boat skimmed swiftly on until we could see, low on the horizon, the dark outline of Cayemitte Island rising above the snowy crests of the breakers. My thoughts turned back to the days when the old sea-dogs, Spanish and French, noblemen by birth and adventurers by profession, had made their headquarters in these romantic waters. They had been a strange mixture of chivalry and savagery, choosing adventure and discomfort rather than an easy life at home. They lived on wild animals whose flesh they dried in strips (boucan) for food at sea, and their daring piracies made these "buccaneers" as notorious as they were infamous. They were the "hi-jackers" of the Spanish Main, preying upon the rich treasure galleons from Peru, and, when opportunity offered, upon their weaker brethren. . . .

Near Coraïl there used to be a gold mine. When the insurrection against King Christophe broke out, a Jesuit Father blasted in the mouth of the mine in order to protect it against the rebels; and he did it so successfully that the entrance was not only impenetrable but entirely concealed. Ensuing generations forgot that the mine ever existed.

Many years later, in fact centuries later, a bibliophile who was browsing through the library of a certain monastery in France, came upon an old parchment manuscript in which the

Jesuit Father had set down in detail the precautions he had taken to protect the mine. Amongst other things the careful Father wrote that the mine had another, concealed entrance, visible only with the aid of a telescope from the southwest corner of the church tower.

The bibliophile, who was no selfish materialist, announced his discovery to the world, as a result of which a bevy of treasure seekers immediately set out for this new bonanza. Even before their arrival at the island they were quarreling over the division of the booty, and when they landed in Coraïl they made a concerted rush for the church tower. Disappointment awaited them. In vain they raked the countryside with their telescopes and binoculars; in vain they dug and excavated in a hundred different places; nowhere was the mysterious passage to be found. The priest had misled them! Most of the party packed up and went home, but there was one tenacious seeker who was not satisfied that the instructions of the manuscript had been followed correctly. He began to delve into local history, chatting with the natives and the oldest inhabitants. His industry was rewarded, for a priest, on turning up the records of the church, discovered that the tower had originally stood on the *other* side of the nave. A hundred years ago there had been an earthquake and the first tower had collapsed. With true Haitian indolence, the inhabitants had chosen to build a tower on the opposite side, rather than have the trouble of clearing away the old débris.

The hunt began anew. On the place where the old tower had stood the remaining enthusiasts erected a high wooden scaffolding and from this new vantage point a hitherto undiscovered fold in the mountains was revealed. Closer inspection disclosed the entrance to the old mine. . . .

Midnight struck from the church tower. An introductory scale of four bells followed by the resonant beat of the hours. Two minutes later the same chimes were repeated. In response to my obvious astonishment Eugène explained: "Ah, monsieur, in case you don't wake up soon enough and you miss the first few beats, you can count them the second time. *Comprenez?*"

Bizóton.

Anyone who wishes to explore Port-au-Prince thoroughly must not fail to visit that quarter of the town which is meant by sailors when they speak of Haiti as "the most beautiful island on earth" and gesture with their hands outlining a well-proportioned female figure.

That district is, of course, the maze of nameless lanes and alleys down by the harbor, from whose houses the red lights wink at night and where slatternly girls lean invitingly out of the windows or sit on their doorsteps clad only in a flimsy kimono. In fact, the red-lamp quarter of the Antilles seaport.

The sight of a white face in these dingy streets always stirs up the lazy inhabitants to a great show of liveliness. They jump up from their seats and flock out of their miserable, tumble-down houses, offering their carnal wares with a revolting lack of modesty. Every shade of color is to be found amongst the crowd from the pale coffee hue of an octoroon to the jet-black skin of an African negress. Whenever a prospective customer comes into view he is immediately surrounded by a shouting horde of women. The younger and fresher girls push the old-timers out of the way. Impertinent advances and obscene gestures which leave nothing to even the dullest imagination serve to emphasize their verbal proposals. "*Monsieur Beaucoup*—bon maison—encouchez—fifty cents!" . . .

Jensen, who was always eager to show me something new on "his" island, as he called it, invited me one evening to come with him and sample the night life of Haiti. I gladly agreed.

The three of us (Hellas refused to be left at home) roared off in Jensen's car through the dark streets of Port-au-Prince. As soon as the town was left behind we turned sharply downhill following the road to Bizóton. On either side of the highway were rows of mud huts in front of which squatted the motionless figures of natives. The only light was the flickering glow of tiny oil lamps which threw such an unreal shimmer over the whole scene that the road appeared to glide past like a ghostly Appian Way. Loud conversation and laughter rang out from the concealing darkness; the only indication that the black images were really alive.

From out of the distance an object hurtled towards us that looked like a gigantic earthbound, fire-spouting rocket. Men and animals dashed in every direction to get out of the way of the monster which, on closer approach, proved to be a locomotive of the *National Chemin de Fer d'Haiti*, small of stature but making a tremendous clatter and roar as it rolled along its narrow-gauge track at the side of the road. The machine was wobbling dangerously and looked as though at any moment it might leave the rails and take to the air puffing sparks like a sky-rocket!

A few miles further on we pulled up in front of the Seaside Inn, a country club as smart as any in Florida or California. Round the house were broad green lawns dotted here and there with clumps of rustling palm trees. Chinese lanterns hung overhead lit with electric glow-lamps which threw their tinted lights over the smart crowd seated at the little tables. Women in Parisian evening wraps; American officers in faultlessly fitting uniforms; smiling white-coated negroes hurrying along with silvery ice buckets and laden trays. It was certainly the most fashionable resort of the white élite of Port-au-Prince.

A negro orchestra struck up the latest jazz "hit" from New York. Wraps and cloaks were laid aside. Two by two the men and women stood up from their sizzling porterhouse steaks and fried chicken and walked gracefully towards the sprung dance floor laid in the center of the lawn. There they moved across the smooth boards, languidly, with practised poise and infinite ennui as they slowly revolved in time to the ear-splitting cacophony of the band. They were perfect examples of our "higher" civilization, dancing with restraint, unemotional and reserved. "Very nice and proper," I thought, "just like the Flamingo Club in Miami."

But I appeared to be the only one of our party who approved of the entertainment. Jensen tried to suppress a yawn without much success. "Too much formality," he muttered.

"Virtuous elimination of the flesh and the devil—bah!" Hellas, who was even more annoyed and bored than Jensen, could control herself no longer for she burst out: "It's terrible to watch this. You white folk have to take lessons in order to dance and even then you can't do it! We colored people dance naturally. To us dancing is as essential as food and drink. We *can* dance, but no white woman could ever make her body speak in that ancient language that expresses her inmost soul. Come on! If you want to see real dancing come and watch the negroes."

In my heart I agreed with her. There was no point in watching this stilted performance. We paid the bill and left. As we drove along the road we passed a cemetery. The jumble of weird tombstones shone eerily in the chill light of the moon like a city built by mad dwarfs. Hellas giggled and pointed at the graveyard.

"I bet you there's more life in those dead bodies than in all you living white men."

Jensen growled some inaudible retort.

We were evidently nearing our destination, for he slowed down and turned into a narrow jungle track where the car lurched in and out of the ruts on either side. A light shone through the darkness ahead. It came from one of the lower windows of a large wooden house. We drove round to the front and parked the car in an open space. Then we tapped on the door and entered.

The room in which we found ourselves ran nearly the whole length of the ground floor. It was hung with colored lanterns and festooned with garish paper streamers. There were tables ranged round the walls and a wide space in the middle for dancing, considerably larger than the few square feet allowed at the Seaside Inn!

When we came in, the guests, who were all colored and mostly men, were sitting at their tables drinking, while the band had a short rest. (Partners, for the most part, were supplied by the establishment.) At a wink from Jensen we were ushered to a discreet table by the owner of the place, a half-caste who had "shady past" written all over his face. He had only one eye and was consequently known to everyone, including my friend, as "One-eye Joe."

The thoughtful man, seeing I was without a partner, sent along a choice of young ladies who were in permanent attendance at this "bal nègre." They had a fine range of coloring from pale brown to black, and they wore transparent organdie dresses which hung in a straight line à la directoire down to their ankles, and were cut low, so low that their bosoms were proudly and unashamedly displayed! Some of the Creoles had smeared their arms, shoulders, and breasts with a coarse rice-powder, evidently hoping to enhance their powers of coquetry. This vulgar attempt to ape their more civilized sisters had completely the reverse effect, for it contrasted unfavorably the glorious picture they made during the day, when they walked along in the sunshine, head proudly poised, bearing a wide basket of oranges or bananas. At such times they were beautiful bronze statues covered only by the abbreviated chemise that decency demanded. But now—their natural beauty was completely spoiled. Of this they seemed to be supremely unconscious. At any rate they were happy. They moved gayly from table to table amongst the guests, chaffing with old friends or sitting down and introducing themselves to new acquaintances.

Cars were now arriving in an almost continuous stream. From out of them stepped the black aristocracy of Port-au-Prince, men in tail-coats or dinner-jackets and women wearing the latest creations of Patou or Lelong. The tables were nearly all full. Exquisite perfumes filled the air. . . .

The band returned to their places and two mestinos started a soft rhythm on a native marimba. At first the notes were slow and dreamy as if they had just awoken from a long sleep; and then they rose louder and louder to the compelling music of the jungle, one instrument after another joining in, thrilling through the room as the whole orchestra swung into a tropical tango beat. Young negroes with their Port-au-Princesses glided over the highly polished floor. Couples undulated together like the heaving waves of a lagoon, their bodies sinuous as smooth boa constrictors. They moved in complete surrender to the rhythm, not speaking, only dancing, instinctively and passionately. Clutched together in a hot embrace they obeyed the call of their blood. Hellas' eyes sparkled like sapphires as she emptied her champagne glass at a single gulp and drew Jensen out onto the floor.

Six mulattoes plucked at the strings of their guitars, thrumming out a frenzied rumba. A young half-caste girl from Martinique sprang into the room, spinning on her toes and whirling like a dervish. She stopped suddenly and from under a gaily colored bandana her large, childish eyes surveyed the men seated round the walls. Then her delicate body began twisting and writhing in seductive contortions, slowly at first and then faster and faster, working up to a climax of exultation. Round and round, backwards and forwards, from table to table. Her loose blouse opened wide at her throat, showing a long narrow strip of gold-brown flesh.

Still she danced on with untiring energy. The tension in the room was terrific. I knew that the climax had not yet

Young negroes with their Port-au-Princesses glided over the floor

come. What was it to be? With quivering arms raised on high a lightning vibration started by her hips traveled through her body, gliding out from her toes and fingers. Again and again her body rippled.

The maracas filled with pebbles joined in the refrain, beating madly the frenzied staccato of the rumba. The end *must* be near. The strain of waiting and watching coupled with the wild music tautened one's nerves till they seemed at breaking point.

Now—the arms of the dancer dropped and crossed behind her. She bent back her head until it almost touched her backbone and then—with a last desperate jerk—she threw back her shoulders. From her tautly stretched blouse two young breasts sprang out, peeping like inquisitive kittens—and vanished immediately under the protecting silk.

"Ah! Oh!" gasped the crowd, dark eyes blazing with desire.

"*Repetez! Encore bis!*" roared the audience—but the little jungle cat was gone.

The band started off again with a fierce blast from the wind instruments, followed quickly by the shrill tones of clarinets and the chirping of the marimba, contrasting oddly like the harsh call of the toucans and the gentler notes of the bell-birds in a forest symphony. Now the drums took up the lead, slowly submerging the rest of the music in a hollow impulsive rhythm.

A full-blooded negress appeared suddenly in the middle of the room—black, naked, a statue carved from polished ebony miraculously endowed with life. Her short curling hair clung in tight ringlets round her Ethiopian skull, giving the appearance of a miniature beehive. There was carmine rouge smeared on her pulpy lips and on the nipples of her heavy tip-tilted breasts. Great golden earrings glittered against her polished sable neck, sparkling in the lamplight and matching the reflections of her high-heeled slippers. Round her waist a short, all-revealing grass skirt hung from a narrow belt, and jumped up and down with every movement of her hips. Her projecting buttocks swayed and rolled; her stomach undulated and twisted in a wild umbilical dance. She displayed all the unbridled vitality of a young jungle queen resolved and sublimated into swelling waves that rippled snakelike down her pliant body. And yet she was no black goddess of voluptuousness, but only a high-spirited child of nature at play.

There was a moment's relaxation, and then the band let loose a nightmare fusillade of drums and crashing cymbals. A troupe of dancing girls dressed in tinselly flimsies stormed into the room and took up their appointed places between the tables. Another screaming discord evoked by the conductor's convulsive arms electrified the maidens into ecstatic motion. With fingers outspread, their hands twitched in aphrodisiac gestures. Their writhing bodies seemed scarcely connected with their legs. It was a hideous and yet fascinating sight. They shook their heads until it seemed they must fall off; their eyes rolled up till only the whites were visible, and gleaming teeth shone between soft, smiling, blood-red lips. Shrill screams of uncontrolled hysteria burst from their mouths and mingled harshly with the howlings of the music. The atmosphere was even tenser than when the mulatto girl had danced the rumba. The men were all leaning forward,

A full-blooded negress appeared suddenly in the middle of the room

each looking at the girl nearest him. Their lips were drawn back in lascivious grins. I could hear the breath of the man on my right hissing between his clenched teeth. The palms of his hands were wet with sweat. A man across the room had stood up trying to catch hold of a girl. Nobody noticed him. The dance went on. It was attaining its orgiastic culmination. Explosive forces, no longer to be controlled, burst forth, exposing all the horrors and wonders of the sixth day of creation. It was there, open and unconfined; personified in the lusting, dripping bodies of the girls, in their paroxysms of sensuality. Fiercer and fiercer, wilder and wilder, faster and faster, on, on—the whole room was gasping.

Then—in the midst of this jazz furioso a sudden blast of trumpets sounded—the end, finish!

"Bravo! Bravo!! Bravo!!!" shouted the guests. "Oh! Ah! Bravo-o-o!!!!"

Lust like a scarlet mist enveloped the room. The great negro beside me licked his lips and buried his head in his hands. He was alone. . . .

A bottle of champagne had cooled us down. The guests were foxtrotting to a more civilized rhythm and the waiters darted about with a clatter of dishes. "One-Eye Joe" came along to our table and brought with him a slim, bronze Creole girl whom he introduced as "Aurora." Her movements held all the polished perfection of a "Dominicaine," as a prostitute is politely called in Haiti. All the time she was sitting at our table she carried herself with an incomparable grace and an entire lack of self-consciousness. She seemed to incorporate physically the ideal type of West Indian half-caste. Her large eyes, brimming with vitality, like those of a wild animal, stared from under her narrow, sloping forehead at the world around. The contour of her oval face was broken by high jutting cheek bones whose hard outlines betrayed an untamed, even cruel trait in her nature. The soft violet-red lips were slightly parted to show an almost too perfect array of pearly white teeth. Her blue-black hair was naturally curly and fuzzed out like a black halo round her head.

She was undeniably attractive. I wondered to myself whose blood was flowing in the veins of that little she-devil; was it the blood of a spear-brandishing warrior from the Congo, or that of a proud-eyed, red-haired Caribbean king? Or even the truly blue blood of a lace and satin-clad, slave-owning Spanish nobleman? Or again the fiery blood of a deck-pacing, thigh-booted, swaggering pirate captain? Some or all of these had been mixed together in the cocktail-shaker of the West Indies and behold!—Aurora. Strange mixtures of blood, such as have produced a Dumas or a Josephine Beauharnais.

Aurora seemed scarcely to have guessed my thoughts. She smiled alluringly at me as with an elegant gesture she raised the long-stemmed champagne glass to her lips and emptied it. Like an ingenuous child, but, I was sure, calculating the effect, she tapped the empty glass against her teeth until the thin crystal chimed like a bell. All the time her beautiful eyes mocked at me in open invitation.

Her appearance held no suggestion of her native blood—one would have said that her country was Spain or Italy. I realized then that I was sitting opposite one of nature's rare and perfect creations: a woman who in any other country would have been the idol of all men, the furore of the smart sets in the Casino of Juan les Pins or on the Promenade des Anglais at Cannes; in fact, the cynosure of all eyes at any fashionable resort in the world. Instead of which this creature

Electrified into ecstatic motion

would blossom and fade unknown, a dancing-partner in an obscure house of pleasure hidden in the Haitian backwoods. It was tragic to think that this triumph of nature would never have an opportunity of realizing her power or of enjoying her perfection to the full.

The marimba band started a melody of strangely cloying and oppressive rhythm.

A murmur ran round the room: "La Merinque!"

The national dance of Haiti!

Against a background of ponderous vibrations the tune sobbed through the smoky air in a monstrous abortion of the tango. It was a strange dance; it was more than a dance—it was a ritual performance, an ovation to love, the ultimate love symbolized in the pairs of bodies, male and female, so closely entwined as to be almost molten into one by the fierce heat of their desire. They swayed over the floor, flexing this way and that, eyes closed, mouths open, forgetting everything in the rapture of their embrace and the seductive discords of the music.

Aurora asked me to dance; she wanted to teach me the "Merinque." We started across the floor. Her movements were soft and submissive, yielding as if her limbs were swathed in invisible ermine. She talked continuously, giving me instructions as we went along. Her blue-black hair, cut square in the Egyptian style, fell forward till it brushed against my face. I submitted to the close pressure of her arms. Her head lay on my shoulder and I could feel the throbbing of her pulse against my neck. Her gold-bronze finger-nails dug into the palms of my hands and her body pressed ever closer to mine in response to the compelling rhythm. A fierce shudder passed through her limbs. The blood coursed in her cheeks as she whispered into my ear words which poured like molten lava between her scarlet lips. She was repeating the message of the drums—the message of primeval love.

Rich perfume and the powerful negroid odor of her body clouded my senses. We danced on, twisting and gliding, pushing to the end of the room, through bead curtains—and beyond, where discreetly subdued lamps lighted the passage to the upper story . . .

"La Merinque" was over.

VIII. LA FERRIÈRE

HECTOR JONNARD hunched his shoulders.

"Monsieur," he said and his voice was dark with terror, "you're asking *me* to accompany you to La Ferrière and—and *to spend the night there.* Oh, no! It's impossible. No man would do it. No one. . . ."

His voice died away to an almost inaudible whisper and his eyes rounded with fear as if King Christophe, the mighty, the tyrant who had died centuries ago, could still hear every word that was spoken of him and his haunted castle.

"Please, please believe me," he pleaded, "it isn't safe up there. Haven't you heard the terrible stories about La Ferrière? Don't you know that it was built with the bones of his victims, that their blood cemented its walls? Every stone in that accursed building has cost a human life. And in the courtyard of the Citadel lies his body; *only* his body—his ghost still wanders through the long galleries and battlements. It would be madness to spend a night there. Not a native in Haiti would do it—not for all the money in the world. But *you*, you may dare—you are a white man and your Voodoo is stronger than all the evil spirits of La Ferrière.

"And yet—who knows—there *have* been white men who vanished during the night. Their bodies were found days afterwards, crushed to a jelly at the foot of the ramparts. The arm of the tyrant had pushed them over the parapet into space. If you visit the Citadel be careful, monsieur, that you too do not die fighting against the unseen enemy who walks La Ferrière in silence. . . . But I see that your mind is made up, you are determined to go, so please, if you value your life, listen to my advice. Take a prayer-book and a crucifix with you, and then you will be safe from the unknown evil—perhaps!"

I laughed. It was really too funny listening to the melodramatic warning of this serious-faced negro. I had expected better of Hector for he was in all other respects an extremely pleasant and intelligent young man; a law student by profession. And yet for all his eighteen years of culture and learning he was as credulous and full of superstition as the simplest and most uncivilized bush negro in Haiti.

He was as obstinate as a mule. I used every argument at my command to try and drive away the shadows of fear from his face; but with no success. There was one more chance—an appeal to his racial pride. I asked him how on earth the negroes could ever hope to become a cultured and emancipated people when even their leaders possessing so-called intelligence (this was a nasty dig) accepted these ridiculous fairy stories as the brand of truth. Hector flushed. I had scored a hit on his most sensitive spot. He hesitated a little longer but I knew that I had beaten him. At last he shrugged his shoulders resignedly and said that he was prepared—albeit unwillingly—to accompany me to La Ferrière. But on one condition: he must return at nightfall to the little negro village near by. If I was really so foolhardy as to insist on spending the night in La Ferrière, he would fetch me in the morning. I would be well advised to take a bottle of rum with me and not to forget my revolver.

So it was settled. We set out from Cap Haitien by car, bouncing along the atrocious "road" to Milot where we planned to spend the first night. After the first hour's travel I thought we should be lucky to get to Milot within a week. Our progress was a jerky one, rolling out of one pot-hole into another. Every once in a while the car stuck on a ridge with the rear wheels rotating furiously, throwing a cloud of choking dust into the air. At other moments we sank up to the axles in the soft sand and it took ten minutes to fill the hole up with sticks and stones so that the wheels could get a grip again. Hector was thoroughly amused watching my rage increase in geometrical proportion to the number of sand-holes we fell into. After about the twentieth he remarked, quite unnecessarily, that "Haiti was obviously meant for the negroes and not for white men! Besides, the Americans had only to repair the roads and nothing would get stuck. It had evidently never occurred to King Christophe that motor cars would want to use his royal highways or he would most certainly have had them asphalted!" I was *not* amused by this rather forced humor, especially as I could not unburden my mind owing to my mouth being full of sand. I managed to spit out one forceful monosyllable which only made Hector laugh immoderately.

However, somehow or other, we got along according to schedule. Just before Milot the road widened out into a stately thoroughfare with a tall avenue of palms on either side. Along this road Christophe had driven in his golden coach drawn by two Arab stallions, and everywhere he passed the terror-stricken populace had fled into the bush to hide from the sight of their tyrant. Today it was different. Everything that lived and had legs came out of the huts to look at us and gaze fearfully at the strange vehicle that moved of its own accord and at the behest of its white driver.

A mile further on the road came to an end in Milot. A steep slope of jungle rose behind the village and in the jungle, half hidden by the trees, was the royal palace of Sans Souci.

Sans Souci! I gazed speechless.

My doubts were resolved. King Christophe was no madman, he was a genius. Perhaps one of the greatest geniuses the world has ever known.

The view that met my eyes was mighty beyond belief. I could not believe that it really existed. It was an edifice of gigantic proportions, noble in its architectural conception and set against a background of incomparable natural beauty. It was a building that equalled any of the great palaces in the Old World, and which, moreover, was not the outcome of centuries' old culture, but the fancy of a negro slave who could neither read nor write.

Silently I stood, gazing at this wonder of the New World. I could not bring myself to realize that its old-time glory had fallen into decay. It was impossible to stay in the sober present. I saw in spirit Sans Souci standing before me as it stood in the reign of the great king, perfect and complete.

An edifice of gigantic proportions, noble in its architectural conception

Before the main entrance rose four high watch towers, slashed with loopholes, and the road ran between them into the great courtyard. There had been a wrought-iron gate barring the way, a masterpiece of hand forging. But the gate had rusted and long since vanished. . . .

The grass and rank creepers grew unchecked on the castle walls and in the courtyard. The windows and doors gaped like the vacant eyes of a dead man. Anyone could get into the palace now. In the old days Christophe used to have sharp, three-pronged iron barbs strewn about the ground to prevent any of his soft-footed subjects approaching unannounced. A wise precaution in those turbulent times!

I began climbing the ascent to the palace. Halfway up I paused. Here were a few fragments of marble; all that was left of a magnificent fountain. Above the fountain had been a black wooden sun whereon was written in gold lettering "*Je vois tout et tout vois par moi dans l'univers.*"

Two further watch towers guarded this approach. Immediately beyond the fountain was a great high terrace and balustrade, where on specially festive occasions King Christophe used to appear in all his pomp and glory to accept the homage of his people. Above this balcony was a façade of immense French windows. Here were the royal apartments, a billiard room, a banqueting hall, a hall of mirrors with an ornately carved mahogany throne, and quarters for the concubines.

Below my feet, deep hewn in stone and rock, lay the dungeons, whose tragic history surpasses in vileness even the ill-famed oubliettes of medieval Western potentates. Thousands of unhappy victims were tortured to death or left to starve in the evil-smelling cells. Their bones still lie there. No one dares disturb them.

Today the palace is a pitiful pile of crumbling devastation. The staircases have fallen in, the roofing has collapsed, and the floors yawn with fathom-deep fissures. Everywhere lay great heaps of rubble. Insects and parasites fought for domination of the deserted pile. Lianas hung like garlands from the ceiling, creeping hungrily along the walls and floor. Cautiously I tested every foothold before I put my weight upon it. I was afraid of joining the skeletons in the dungeons! Suddenly I stumbled over a heap of tiles and stones that blocked my way and horrible vermin ran out of the débris. Hairy tarantulas, like sponges soaked in black ink, scuttled from hole to hole.

From a bow window I gazed across the landscape spread before me. It was wonderful; there could be no more glorious panorama upon earth. Into the distance stretched the rolling jungle, flaunting every color of the rainbow against its green expanse. The palm trees swayed in a gentle whispering breeze. Far on the horizon sparkled a broad band of limpid lapis lazuli—the Caribbean Sea.

I could imagine the king standing, as he must so often have stood, on this very place, watching with his antique telescope for the approaching ships of unwelcome strangers as they rounded the distant cape. Haiti was taboo for the white man. . . .

A brightly colored butterfly fluttered over my head into the room and settled with outspread wings upon the far wall as if to relieve the bareness with a splash of color. Gobelin tapestries and Old Masters framed in gilt had hung there once!

The king wanted to be civilized and civilization had been his downfall. All the interior decorations to the palace had been done by artists from Hamburg. Every conceivable luxury had been installed in Sans Souci. Amongst other things Christophe had caused a mountain stream to be diverted into pipes which ran under the marble flooring and kept the palace cool. There was an immense and comprehensive library, to what purpose no one knew for the king could neither read nor write. There was also a court printing press. Most of the books printed there have vanished. Now and again a copy may be found in one of the island libraries. I remembered the volume I had discovered in the seminary at Jérémie. It was a play which the author had dedicated to his queen, the wife of Christophe. The title was:

NERI

Chef des Haitiens

Tragedie en trois actes, par son Excellence le Comte de Rosiers

On the fly-leaf were written the words of a then popular song:

C'est trop long temp souffrir, chére amie,
C'est trop long temp souffrir, chére amie,
C'est trop long temp souffrir
Pour mes premières amours.

Adieu, chére amie, pour toujours,
Adieu, chére amie, pour toujours,
Adieu, ma chére amie,
L'objet des mes amours.

The man who wrote these verses must have been deeply in love and seemingly thought that loving phrases must be repeated several times before they attain the desired effect! Perhaps the author had directed the effusions of his pen at

Madame Christophe, in which case he was a wise man to surrender his amour. Queens are notoriously dangerous people to love!

The castle even had its own mint. Christophe, however, only allowed six gold pieces to be coined bearing the impress of his own head, the rest bore the crest of Haiti. Of these six, one is in the Viennese Numismatic Collection to which it was presented by Karl Ritter, who in turn got it from his friend the Duke of Marmalade.

In the east wing of the palace I visited the ruins of the great cruciform chapel. Its walls have crumbled away, the altars are empty, and the saints have long since vanished from their niches. On the broad terrace running the whole length of one side of the palace there still stands the vast mango tree beneath whose shade Christophe, as first and only judge in the land, sat and pronounced judgment over life and death. The dust is dry that once was clotted with blood and the names of the countless heads which rolled on the ground before his black majesty are forgotten. Under the same tree I rested. The air was fresh and deep peace such as it had never known in its lifetime lay over the ruins of the palace. Thousands of yellow butterflies swayed in the sunlight. Green lizards darted across the ground at my feet.

It was growing towards evening. Hector had left, saying he would be ready to continue our journey at seven o'clock the next morning. Amongst the huts scattered at the foot of Sans Souci there were signs of reawakening animation. Four goats climbed up to the castle walls to enjoy the cool evening air and snatch a few mouthfuls of tasty leaves. Hens, followed by their numerous brood, perambulated the courtyard and terrace, cackling proudly. A fat negress, panting and cursing, chased a squealing piglet round and round a watch tower.

The peace was broken; it was time I left and inquired for a night's lodging.

One of the huts in Milot was called "Café St. Marie." It was the largest building in the village and looked as though it might possess a spare bed. The proprietress, a fat and none too cleanly negress, received me with great hospitality and showed me into the back room where stood a ramshackle iron bedstead. After a close examination, hygienic and zoölogical, I hired both bed and room for the night. From the counter in the shop I bought some cassava bread and tinned fruit in addition to which the good woman produced from the depths of her cellar a solitary bottle of Patzenhofer Export beer. I bought this too, for the price of three gourdes (about 50 cents). The stale atmosphere in the café was not conducive to an appetite so I retired outside and made an excellent supper off my purchases. Although no ice was to be had, the beer tasted quite passable after it had been left to cool for half an hour in a near-by stream. When I had finished the food and drink I lit a cigarette and strolled back to the palace again. The night was too wonderful to be indoors and I sat on the terrace until long past midnight.

Early the next morning I was up, dressed, and ready to depart. Tinned fruit and bread again formed my hasty breakfast, for I was afraid of missing the horses which the Préfet of Milot had promised me would arrive at six o'clock to take us to La Ferrière. I was a fool and I should have known better. Seven o'clock—and there was still no sign of my Rosinante. Half-past seven—Hector was conspicuous by his absence. Eight o'clock—I opened another tin of apricots and lay down on my bed again. I indulged in philosophic thought; if one is in no hurry and has enough patience, all things come to him who waits—even in Haiti. Trite but true!

At half-past eight Hector strolled in and greeted me with the most charming smile. There was obviously no hope of getting off before mid-day so we sat down to a leisurely breakfast; my second, or was it third? The coffee and eggs were delicious, so delicious that all my impatience vanished and I was content to bask in the sunshine in front of the Café St. Marie, chatting to Hector and waiting for something to happen.

At nine o'clock three horses came into view on the broad road below. They were led by three soldiers who were not hurrying themselves. Hence the delay! The troop approached at a snail's pace and even when they did arrive the soldiers were unwilling to hand over our prospective mounts. However, the musical clink of a few coins and the sight of my permission to visit the Citadel issued by the gendarmerie and heavily weighted with the official seals eventually convinced them of our *bona fides*. Having done their duty they vanished into the café to spend their *baksheesh*.

Hector roped our luggage onto the pack-saddle which one of the horses carried and we mounted the other two nags. At half-past nine, only three and a half hours late, our little cavalcade clip-clopped over the cobblestones, soon leaving the village and the precincts of Sans Souci far behind.

After a few minutes' ride the palace and the broiling sun were both hidden from view. We trotted along the dark, moss-grown path that led to La Ferrière. Dark, because the jungle arched and laced overhead, forming a thick roof through which only a dim gray glimmer of light penetrated.

A steamy twilight enfolded us. The ground under foot became boggier and boggier, and sometimes the path closed in so much that we had to lie flat on our horses' necks in order to pass beneath the low-hanging branches. When the undergrowth became too thick to push aside, machetes came into play and we hacked our way through. Now and again our enthusiasm (I doubt if Hector ever had any for this expedition!) was damped by our horses falling into bog holes up to their bellies. On these occasions we had to dismount and haul the wretched animals out by dint of brute force.

Green snakes with flickering tongues gazed inquisitively down at us from the broad palm leaves overhead and then rustled off into the bush. Hector informed me with some diffidence that these reptiles were sacred to Voodoo and therefore inviolable.

Somewhere among the trees rang the clear, bell-like song of a bird. Two more joined in; one whistling discordantly like a high-spirited errand boy, and the other hammering away like a smith on his anvil.

We rode round a giant fern which grew in the middle of our path, and came face to face with a clear stream of water springing from a craggy face of rock. This was as unexpected as it was welcome. We dismounted and drank long cool draughts and felt much better. Even the horses, who had followed our example, seemed refreshed, for they ambled on a little quicker through the stifling jungle.

As we advanced the vegetation became denser. Trees in fantastic shapes such as are only to be found in the tropics loomed up around us. The forms they grew in were so grotesque and nightmarish that I gasped with astonishment and not a little fright every time a new one came into view. Little birds, vividly plumaged but quite songless, darted out of the thickets and flitted to and fro for a few moments before vanishing again between the dark trees.

A quarter of an hour later the path widened into a clearing and Hector and I had just dismounted for a brief rest when something large and shimmering plunged from above and hovered before my face. For one moment I was completely dazzled. It seemed to me that a piece of pure blue sky had come unstuck from its place in the firmament and fallen to earth. I blinked in amazement. Never before had I seen such a butterfly. I raised my hand, but luckily for him I hesitated. To grasp at the glorious creature would only be to spoil his beauty. Every time a ray of sunlight touched his wings there came a blinding flash of radiance. For a long second he hovered. Then he was gone. But the sight had so impressed itself on the retina of my eyes that I could still see the flash and glitter long after the butterfly himself had vanished.

The way was climbing steadily. The sharp sweet smell of decay and death filled the air. A flock of birds rose shrieking at our approach, disturbed from their feast of rotting flesh. A hundred yards ahead the jungle lightened and we entered an open space where lay scattered half-a-dozen palm-thatched huts.

The natives came out and stared at us in surly silence. At length in response to Hector's persistent questioning some food was produced, and an old white-haired negro came forward and introduced himself as Bonhômme Guamba, guardian of the Citadel. After a meal consisting of chicken, roast bananas, and palm wine we joined Guamba who, garrulous with alcohol, began to talk about La Ferrière.

"Do you know," he whispered confidingly, "that La Ferrière is built entirely of stone as big as this"— he stretched his arms as wide apart as possible to illustrate the marvel.

I remarked that it must have been hard work to get them into position.

"Ah, monsieur," he answered, "no man could move such stones. . . ." And as if fearing some ghostly wrath the old man glanced nervously round before continuing.

"Christophe the King sat on the terrace of Sans Souci, playing his bamboo flute. At every note that Christophe blew a block of stone loosed itself from the cliff side, grew wings and flew away to La Ferrière. Again at the king's command, each stone sank into its appointed place and shed its wings like an ant. Naturally, without their wings the stones couldn't move any more. You can still see them up there. La Ferrière still stands today!" He concluded with a triumphant gesture.

I could well understand La Ferrière still being there, but I made no comment on his story. In some curious way it rang true. So I thanked him for his information and gave him a few gourdes to look after our horses. Then we started off towards our final destination. As soon as the old man saw where we were going, he ran after us, explaining that no strangers were allowed to visit the Citadel unaccompanied by him, the official guide. I had no wish to be "guided" so I bought him off and sent him back to the village. At last Hector and I were alone, on the last lap, bound for La Ferrière.

The Haitian Government is nowadays extremely apprehensive of letting visitors examine the ruins unaccompanied and unwatched. They have a very good reason for this.

Some decades ago a mulatto sat in a low drinking house by the harbor. He called for his bill, which was a fairly large one, for he had been there since early morning and was now hopelessly drunk, and to the host's astonishment he paid for the wine with bright Spanish doubloons. On being questioned he stated that his wealth came from Christophe's treasure house in La Ferrière. This admission came out in a moment of drunken confidence, but he soon realized that he had said a great deal too much. Neither cursing nor cajoling could persuade him to utter another word on the subject. The police now arrived on the scene and tried what a little persuasion could do. They too were unsuccessful; prison and beatings were a failure as a means of loosening the man's tongue. He refused to give any more information.

Then the government decided to act on their own initiative. They sent a company of soldiers together with the most reliable officers in the army to explore the fortress. The search lasted for months—and nothing was discovered; not a glint of gold was to be seen.

It was well known and an authentic historical fact that Christophe just before his death had all his treasure, one and a half million pounds worth, conveyed to La Ferrière, where it was hidden in a specially constructed chamber. The careful tyrant further arranged that all the soldiers who transported the gold, and who consequently were the only people besides the king to know its hiding place, never returned alive. His precautions were successful. Not even the government of Haiti with all its resources behind it could unearth one doubloon of Christophe's precious wealth. And by all accounts his ghost still guards it today!

The mulatto who was the cause of all this excitement is still living in the island, but he has never revealed the source of his prosperity.

Hence the cautious attitude of the government towards strangers who wish to explore La Ferrière alone!

Before we set out, Hector and I packed a few necessities into our rucksacks, not forgetting a pair of thick blankets, for the night in the mountains is apt to be very cold. The first and hardest part of our climb led up and over the chalk ridge of Bonnet l'Evêque. During the ascent which was steep and tiring I pulled myself up by means of overhanging plants and branches. All the time I had to keep a sharp lookout for small snakes against which Bonhômme had specially warned me. He said that their bite meant certain death unless the victim had the presence of mind to cut deep into the wound and cauterize it immediately. Even this drastic treatment would not stave off a long and painful illness. Hector and I kept a careful watch but luckily we did not see a single reptile.

Suddenly the trees and jungle fell back. We had passed the upper limit of vegetation and emerged on the bare mountain side. It was sensibly colder and a sharp wind blew across from Santo Domingo. As a final deterrent a thick wet mist came down, so enshrouding us that I could scarcely see Hector although he was only a few paces in front of me. Clouds swept round the summit and a fierce storm of icy hail rattled down. We squatted on the ground and got what protection we could by spreading the blankets over our heads. If any negroes had happened to come along they certainly would not have paused to examine these "fetishes" before running away. I smiled at the thought of what a curious sight we must be, peering out from beneath our blankets. But there was no chance of anyone coming by. Here was nothing but the dreariest wastes; no negro would dare to walk upon the Bonnet l'Evêque, not even in broad daylight. Only we were there—alone with the elements.

After an unpleasant quarter of an hour the hail stopped. The contrast was eerie in the extreme. Before, there had been the friendly pattering of the stones, but now there was complete, blanketing silence, broken only by the steady dripping of the water.

Then the lowering clouds divided and the summit appeared, bathed in the golden glory of a blazing sun.

I looked upwards. Perched on the mountain peak, itself a mighty rock, there towered—tremendous and appalling—the Citadel of King Christophe.

My awe and amazement was even profounder than on the day before when I had first seen Sans Souci. With the palace it had been the architecture that had so impressed me. But now—now it was the fulfillment of a conception, the embodiment of a stupendous imagination, the solid fact as it stood . . . so vast that no words could encompass it. Of such grandeur that all description is beggared.

The first thought that flashed through my brain was: How could it be? How could *Man* have built this fortress here in the depths of the wilderness, in the heart of the jungle, on the slippery peak of a precipitous mountain, the climbing of which had taken me, with practically no luggage, a good three weary hours? A fortress whose impregnability was as perfect as an irresistible truth. A miracle on earth. . . . It was beyond belief.

A *Will* had built that fortress; a Will perhaps stronger even than Napoleon Bonaparte's whose army it had conquered. La Ferrière was a concrete realization of the dreams and ambition of an unknown negro slave.

King Christophe commanded—and La Ferrière arose. One command!—and a hundred thousand men pulled and hauled and pushed and lifted a hundred thousand tons of stone. Upwards—ever higher and higher, up to the summit! But it was not always the *same* men who strained at the ropes; many thousands sank dying by the way; countless

Perched on the mountain peak—tremendous and appalling—the Citadel of King Christophe

victims fell to the whip and the bullet that always threatened the exhausted men. . . . But every stone reached its appointed place. Bonhômme Guamba had been right with his little fable. The legend of the winged rocks which obeyed the king's command had a deeper and a truer meaning than I had ever realized.

And so La Ferrière was built. But more terrible than the haulage of the great stone blocks was the bringing of the three hundred and fifty bronze cannon and guns of the heaviest caliber which were destined for the defense of the ramparts. And when these were in place there came mountains of ammunition and food and other necessities for the garrisoning of the Citadel. It was a superhuman undertaking and yet every pound of stone and iron and powder was brought by the hand of man, on a human back—costing human blood. . . .

Look along the walls! This was no barbarian edifice with blocks piled loosely one on top of another. Every stone had been built in and cemented into place. A genius at building fortifications had designed it; a genius certainly, but also an architect of unrivaled ability, for the mountain and the Citadel seemed welded into one as if the living rock itself had opened up and crowned the mountain with a titanic helmet.

Hector stood beside me and enjoyed my amazement. He plainly took it as a well-earned compliment to himself and his people.

I walked round the base of the wall, Hector following. He had a horror of the building and made no attempt to conceal it. If La Ferrière had seemed immense from a distance, now under its very shadow it was colossal beyond imagination. I stopped for a moment and gazed up.

I looked up the massive smooth walls of La Ferrière. Perpendicular they rose, almost to the blue sky. And in the sky were a few white clouds sailing along, gently and very slowly. But—my heart leapt into my throat—it was *not* the clouds which were moving, it was la Ferrière itself, gradually and ever so surely leaning further and further out, with all those hundreds of thousands of tons of stone waiting to fall on me. A scream died in my throat. I was hypnotized by the black rim of the wall as it moved across the snowy patch of cloud—towards me, waiting to crash and bury me in its fearful collapse. . . .

Hector grasped my arm and I looked down at the ground, dizzy with fright. We walked on in silence.

At last we reached a high, rusty iron door, the only means of access to the fortress. It hung slightly open and, as I pushed, it swung right back, squeaking on its hinges until the ghastly noise reverberated through the building like a giant's laughter. A hand grabbed my wrist and dragged me back. It was Hector! His face had turned several shades paler to an octoroon shade.

"*Attention*, monsieur!" he whispered and his low voice was worse than the creaking of the hinges for it echoed in a low-pitched titter round the empty corridors. "*Attention.* There are dangerous depths and abysms in there. You will fall to your death if you don't guard every footstep." I whispered back that I would be careful, and we stepped into the dark interior. . . .

A murky labyrinth of passages and rooms stretched away before me. The muzzles of heavy cannon stuck out from the embrasures dominating the desolation against an enemy that had never come—that never would come.

Sharply outlined circles of sunlight pierced through the

apertures set in the yard-thick wall, shining into the twilit casemates and glinting on the bronze barrels of the guns. I deciphered with difficulty the lettering embossed on the metal. On one twenty-four pounder it read: "*Georgius IV Rex*"; another bore the "*N*" of the great Napoleon; and yet another was christened "*El Sabio*," the Sage.

A number of the cannons still rested on their old wooden gun-carriages, others lay around on the stone floor as if some giant hand had scattered them there. One or two barrels wore long gray beards of stalactites, grown from the constant water drippings of a century. In the darkness I stumbled over some cannon balls which lay strewn about behind the battery. And then I noticed a perfect pyramid of ammunition and I had the fleeting impression that the black gunners could only have piled it yesterday. Every cannon stood in its own embrasure, each one separated from the other by a thick protecting wall so that, in case of a direct hit or an explosion in one casemate, the others would be shielded from danger.

In 1817, during a thunderstorm, a flash of lightning struck the powder room, which blew up destroying, amongst others, Prince Noel, who was stationed there at the time. It testifies to the immense strength of the fortress that the whole building was not shattered by the force of this tremendous explosion.

Most of the arches in the galleries were built without keystones. Each stone in the vaulting had been symmetrically diminished to the accuracy of a hair's breadth until it fitted into the complete arch; a great feat of construction. One room which we entered contained huge casks of damp but still serviceable gunpowder. Along the walls were a great many holes dug by greedy treasure seekers. Evidences of their activities were also shown by the iron-bound chests with the lids blasted open which blocked the passage in several places. We clambered over these and went on, climbing from gallery to gallery, higher and higher. By the side of the steps I noticed cunningly contrived niches, probably built for the disposal of undesirable intruders. Our footsteps raised an eerie, muffled echo. Bats flitted away, rustling close by my face. Rats squeaked in the darkness. . . .

Hector followed behind and every now and then he clutched at my arm in a spasm of fright. I was not feeling too confident myself, and it annoyed me to have a hand clawing at me unexpectedly. However, I said nothing for I was grateful for his company. Carefully—step by step—we groped our way through the gloomy half-light of the endless corridors. I was glad of my electric torch, for its steady beam on the uneven floor revealed many unexpected stairs and several yawning shafts which seemed to sink into the very bowels of the mountain.

A chill moisture impregnated the air. Water trickled down the slimy walls and pallid fungi sprouted from every crevice. I was suddenly afraid of getting lost for we had twisted and turned and climbed so many staircases that I doubted whether we should ever be able to retrace our steps. However, it was too late now to take any precautions so we went on. Then we came to another long room in which were piled great heaps of ancient flintlocks. I explored round and at the farther end my torch lighted on an opening in the wall where a passage led steeply downwards. I was determined to discover what lay at the end. Perhaps there was a vague idea in my mind that I would find heaps of gold but I realized quickly enough that this would be one of the first places that the keen-eyed seekers would search. Still, there might be something interesting in there. Hector firmly refused to come with me. He said he would wait for me in the long room. So he seated himself on a pile of flintlocks and produced a box of matches against my departure with the torch.

The passage seemed interminable. It wound first to the right and then to the left, and then to the right again in a serpentine fashion, evidently running inside one of the great walls. After about five minutes' cautious progress the roof sloped sharply down and there was a dead end. I flashed my torch about. The passage must obviously lead somewhere or it would never have been built. There seemed to be a dark shadow on the ground in front of the blank wall and on closer examination I discovered it to be a hole, about three feet in diameter, which gave on a flight of spiral steps. I started to descend, one hand pressed against the outer wall to steady myself and the other shining the torch on each step before I tested it. Round and round the staircase went until I became so dizzy that I had to sit down. When I went on, I redoubled my caution for it occurred to me that the steps might end in a sudden shaft to destroy the unwary stranger. However, they eventually came to an end in front of an iron door which barred my further advance.

There was a bolt on the outside. I pulled with all my weight and it moved back. The hinges were rusted almost solid and screamed like a thousand devils in torment when I heaved at the door. Then it swung open unexpectedly and I stumbled forward into pitch darkness. I dropped my torch but luckily it fell unbroken. I bent and picked it up. The air was almost unbreathable. No one could have been here since Christophe died. All round the walls there hung down heavy chains and at various heights iron rings were let into the stonework. The floor was covered with mildew.

This must be one of the deepest dungeons in the fortress. How many men had been buried alive here—so near the laughing sunshine and flowering orange trees. The stones were silent: they would not tell how many victims of the tyrant had lain here, without light, without air, and screamed and screamed until they were dead. . . .

I had seen enough, so I rejoined Hector and together we climbed onto the stone roof of La Ferrière. It was sectioned in such a way that, in case of siege, it could be used as a rainwater cistern. Gutters led the water across the flat stone into holes which were situated directly over gigantic tanks on the floor below. Christophe had thought of everything!

I stood entranced with the beautiful panorama spread before me. It was a well earned recompense for all the dreary darkness inside the Citadel. Below us lay a wild range of mountains; a vista of deep valleys and high precipices. At the foot of the Bonnet l'Evêque stretched the jungle out of whose green depths peeped a few negro huts. Above, white clouds chased through the sky and underneath their shadows crept across the rocks and trees. Westwards lay Santo Domingo; in the distance gleamed the blue Caribbean. All around was silence.

I felt as though I were perched on the top of the world. Actually I was standing on one of the highest peaks of the Antilles, that immense chain of mountains of which only the very summit appears above the sea and whose tops alone form this group of islands where dwell more than fifteen million inhabitants. From the bottom of the Caribbean Sea to La Ferrière where I was lay a difference of altitude exceeding even the great Gaurisankar Deep.

And still I stood on the battlements of the Citadel and marveled at the architect who created it. The whole fortress was irregular in design as the lay of the ground had demanded; no two towers were alike, and yet the building was a perfect unity. The north tower was the dominant feature, reaching up like a ship's prow into the clouds.

Even today La Ferrière stands supreme. Time and the elements have laid Sans Souci in ruins. La Ferrière is still indomitable. It has withstood the storms and revolutions of a century. The earthquake of 1842 tore a great crack in the walls of the north tower and the red moss clings to the bleached stones like blood oozing out of a wound. But its ancient strength is still undiminished; it will weather many centuries more. . . .

I wandered along the highest edge of the roof. Here the walls rose sheer from a deep precipice, forming a perpendicular drop into the gray depths below. I threw a heavy stone over and listened . . . not a sound. Then—long seconds after—I heard a faint echo rise from the valley below.

Today I could walk here unmolested; no treacherous hand would hurl me to my death. It had been one of King Christophe's favorite amusements to take some man who had displeased him out on to the roof to look at the beautiful view. The unsuspecting one stood lost in admiration and then—a gentle push—and he toppled over to be dashed to pieces on the sharp rocks below. A very satisfying form of vengeance!

Once, when the English ambassador paid an official visit to La Ferrière, the king decided to show his guest the perfect discipline of his army by making a platoon of soldiers march up and down the parapet.

His Majesty himself gave the commands.

"Right wheel . . . left wheel . . . steady . . . about turn . . . FORWARDS!!"

The platoon advanced in perfect step, straight on, unhesitating—over the edge. Rank after rank vanished silently into the depths.

It was fear that built La Ferrière. Fear for one man who held the whole nation under his sway. Fear built La Ferrière and brutality was its architect. Without these two driving passions the Citadel could never have arisen. The king commanded and the whips of plaited cowhide lashed unmercilessly until man or matter had to give way. One or the other, *he* did not mind which. Thousands died, but there were still thousands more to take their place. Life was no object. Man triumphed. And in less than four years the masterpiece was completed. It was truly a memorial of blood.

I took my bearings from the roof and then climbed down in the direction of the courtyard. More by good luck than any skillful memorizing of the way I reached the yard without getting lost once. Then I pushed through the six-foot quingo grass and past the sweet-smelling tamarinds until I reached the middle. There stood the grave of Christophe the Great; a little rectangular house with steeply sloping eaves. The pale pink walls were blotched with hideous patches of decay. At the head of the tombstone gaped a wide hole where some desecrator had dug for treasure. An orange tree spread its branches, heavily laden with ripe fruit, over the grave. The tyrant slept in peace.

Hours had passed since I first entered the Citadel. It was already evening, so Hector took his leave, saying he would stay in the village below and wait till I turned up on the

I wandered along the highest edge of the roof

morrow. I almost said I would go with him, for now that I had seen La Ferrière I was not tempted to spend the night in the place, but since I wanted to finish off a few sketches the next morning I said nothing. Besides I had to prove to him *ad oculos* the superiority of the white man. So I stuck to my original plan.

I pitched my camping place beside the king's grave where I cleared the ground and spread out the few blankets which formed my bed.

After a short tropical twilight darkness fell. The stars shone brightly in the clear sky above. Gradually my eyes became accustomed to the gloom and I was soon able to distinguish my surroundings.

The wind suddenly got up and howled and sang through the empty rooms and along the corridors like some ghostly organ played by phantom hands. Loud bangs echoed from the walls.

The loneliness weighed heavily upon me. I lit a fire, unpacked the cooking utensils, and began preparing my evening meal. When I had finished I sat with my back against the miniature house and sniffed the delicious aroma of strong Haitian coffee. A sound came from the grave behind me. It was only the wind but it sounded like an agonized groan.

No need for fear. The king slept peacefully. . . .

IX. KING CHRISTOPHE OF HAITI

As I sat in the fitful glow of my campfire I thought of the wonders I had seen during the day, and I thought more especially of their creator. *Tout passe. . . .* Today the world has all but forgotten the great ruler whose dust lay beneath the shabby tombstone at my back.

Round about his last resting place towers La Ferrière, the child of his brain, which will outlive him by thousands of years and in which *he* will live for centuries to come. For La Ferrière is Christophe's true memorial; it is no mausoleum for the dead, but a temple for the living, for the indomitable spirit which once inhabited a black body called Henri Christophe. The king built Sans Souci for his pleasure and pride. It lies in ruins. But the Citadel, *his* Citadel, he built for himself, a lasting monument of his majestic greatness.

Alone and dark, gigantic and tyrannical, the creation mirrors the creator. The king, the man of flesh and blood, has found his reincarnation in La Ferrière, the Cyclopean rock that stretches up to heaven. Further from man and nearer to the sun than anywhere else in Haiti, Christophe dreams his last dream.

In him, its greatest and most gifted leader, the black race attained its highest form of expression. He is the personification of all that is wonderful and all that is terrible in the negro people, and therefore he remains an incomprehensible enigma to the white man.

But nevertheless much can be learned from the history of Christophe and the deeds of the king must lay hold on our imagination and fill us with breathless amazement.

Somewhere in the West Indies—in a wretched little hut on a sugar plantation—a black slave mother, the wife of a slave father, gave birth to a little slave son.

That was in the year 1767 and his parents christened him Henri Christophe. The plantation owner would have rather had a new foal, for the baby was a nuisance in his eyes. He kept his mother from at least one day's work when he was born and he was only an encumbrance after that.

Therefore, when the boy was eight years old, his white master sold him to a fisherman. Christophe was a good worker but the fisherman could not really afford to keep an assistant so he disposed of him to the innkeeper at Cap Haitien. At first he worked as a stableboy, forbidden to come into the house, but he proved to be an intelligent lad, so after some years he was promoted to the post of barman.

Here, in a dark drink-sodden room he served the sailors who came up from the ships lying in the harbor below. He was only twelve now, but he was eager to hear about the world and he listened avidly to these men of many nationalities, absorbing all they had to say and learning many of their languages. In fact the tap-room taught him all that he would have learned at school, that is excepting reading and writing which he never achieved during the whole course of his life.

As Christophe developed into manhood, his consuming hatred of the white race grew in proportion to his body. He hated above all the aristocratic man for whom his parents had slaved, and who had sold him away from his mother and father like a piece of useless cattle flesh. And he hated as well the foul-mouthed sailors whom he had to serve and cringe to while they cursed him as a "filthy nigger" in their drunken frenzies. This hatred was the mainspring of his life. But as yet he was helpless to avenge the insults to his people. He waited patiently.

Then the Bastille fell in Paris. Sailors brought the news to Haiti and they shouted the rousing words: "*Liberté, Egalité, Fraternité.*" They told of Robespierre the patriot and of the guillotine swimming in the blood of the aristocracy. They sang the *Marseillaise* and Christophe gloried in the words of freedom, repeating them to himself until the refrain was seared into his soul:

Qu'un sang impur
Abreuve nos sillons.

"When the blood of tyrants flows our seed shall sprout. . . ."

Those were the days when the seed was sown, and Christophe knew it. He knew that the seed was sown deep within him, but did he know that out of this unsavory drinking house in Cap Haitien a champion of the negroes would arise who was to be the equal of Robespierre and Napoleon? Perhaps he already realized what was to come.

Slowly the seed ripened.

But first there was trouble between the white men themselves. Seventy thousand white men fought one another. Unity, their one great strength against the blacks, had failed.

The opportunity was missed. There came a new régime; freedom for the seventy thousand whites to whom the land belonged, freedom for the twenty thousand half-castes born of a black mother and fathered by a white man, but slavery, unending slavery, for the five hundred thousand unhappy negroes . . . *that* was justice in Haiti under the new régime.

It was too much to be borne. Three great leaders of the people arose, Christophe, Toussaint l'Ouverture, and Dessalines. They raised the standard of revolt. The flames of rebellion roared red above the housetops and blood ran scarlet in the streets. But the madness had not spread; there was still time for a peaceable agreement, and Toussaint, the idealist, sought to bring it about. Fearlessly he went to Napoleon, the raiser of the tricolor, the champion of freedom, and he begged for the liberation of black Haiti. The answer he got was decisive and he tasted a sample of Napoleon's treachery in a French prison.

There was now no other way left open. Violence was the only answer, violence and unspeakable atrocities. Dessalines led the maddened negroes against the whites. He exacted a terrible vengeance from France. Every white man must die, every half-caste must die, Haiti is for the blacks alone! That was their slogan and they fulfilled it to the very letter. They tore the white strip from the French *tricouleur*, and proclaimed red and blue the national colors of Haiti. The land was theirs. They had turned it into a shambles at the word of their leader. Now they hoped for peace.

Then Dessalines the Butcher fell at the hands of the assassin. One man was left in all Haiti fit to rule his people.

That man was Christophe.

Christophe was left; the last of the three great fighters. He had learned wisdom from the mistakes of the other two. Dessalines had called himself "Emperor"; Christophe was content, for the time being at least, with the title of "President."

He had a big task before him. Chaos reigned throughout the land, the money bags were empty, the emancipated slaves were starving—and the French still howled their fearful threats of vengeance.

There was no choice. From the very beginning, Christophe *had* to be a tyrant.

First find bread. The President declared all wild gourds state property. Every Haitian must deliver them, as many as he could gather, to the nearest collecting station. The negroes were astonished and many rebelled. Every discontent died a horrible death. The people obeyed.

Gourds[1] are to the Haitian what daily bread is to the white man—and much more, for when the inside has been eaten, the hard skin serves for plates, spoons, bottles, boxes, and a hundred other necessities of life. Christophe knew that. He did not keep the gourds for himself but he exchanged

[1]Gourds, a name given to various plants of the order *Cucurbita* and *Lagenaria*. Its cultivation began far beyond the dawn of history.

It contains a considerable amount of nutriment and the fruit can be kept even in a warm climate for a long time.

The deep yellow flesh of the *Cucurbita* can be cooked and eaten. The hard-skinned *Lagenaria* or bottle gourds are cultivated for ornament and because their excavated shells are useful as dippers, dishes, etc.—*Encyclopaedia Britannica.*

Fear must be planted in the people. Fear made them docile, and through fear they could achieve the impossible

them with his subjects in return for coffee, cotton, and other tropical products. The new ruler set out to educate his people as productive farmers. The raw stuffs he received he sold to the foreigner for cash. From gourds came coffee, from coffee came gold, and that is why the money of Haiti today is called "gourdes."

This simple economic plan was extraordinarily effective. Haiti became richer than ever before. The people were contented and the country was now ripe for Christophe the King. On June 2, 1811, the forty-four-year-old negro was crowned "King Henri" by a French bishop.

The first act of the sovereign was to formulate the *Code Henri*—a law of work by whose enactment every adult man and woman was compelled to do at least fourteen hours' labor every day.

Undreamt-of prosperity was the result. Ships carried Haiti's exports over the Seven Seas. Scholars and diplomats of all nations came to pay their respects to the black king. National schools were founded throughout the land, where presided white teachers specially selected by the king. Christophe wanted to have an educated people; he wanted to give to the youth of Haiti the opportunities *he* had never had. In those days he was almost a benevolent tyrant.

Every morning and every afternoon the king rode out from the palace accompanied by a page-boy carrying a telescope. Often the horses pulled up. The page handed over the telescope and through it Christophe would study the surrounding countryside. Woe to the person who was seen lazing in front of his hut. A cruel whipping soon persuaded him that it was better to work than to dream the day away. If it was a woman she suffered the same punishment.

Fear must be planted in the people. Fear made them docile,

and through fear they could achieve the impossible. A new reign of terror had begun.

On one of the highest mountains in Haiti, King Christophe built an eternal monument to fear—La Ferrière.

The Citadel was to be a lasting memorial to his might and a protection for the people of the plain. It would threaten far out to sea any unwelcome strangers whose thoughts might turn to conquest or invasion. It was to be the symbol of Haiti—and her king.

The difficulties that beset the builders were almost insuperable. Tens of thousands of men succumbed. Every available worker was recruited. The king himself assisted, laying on mortar with a trowel. Three hundred and fifty heavy cannons were drawn up the steep mountain-side by man power alone. The whips lashed pitilessly across the blood- and sweat-streaked backs of the human animals. The demands upon their strength were more than flesh and bone could stand. Their muscles tore and snapped, but the great cannon would not move.

"It is too heavy for us! We *cannot* go on!" screamed the exhausted men as they sank down on the slippery face of rock. It was true; they *could* not go on, and as the barbed whips tore great gaping wounds they only moaned and crouched closer to the earth.

With a harsh voice the king ordered the men to line up before him. They could not stand, but they were propped against the cannon which they had failed to move. Then Christophe walked slowly down the row. Every third man he shot. The cannon reached the top.

La Ferrière was finished. In his heart of hearts Christophe regarded it as a last sanctuary in time of trouble. But miles of forest separated it from his palace of Sans Souci and therefore a secret passage, deep underground, was dug between the two. As soon as this was completed all the workmen were strangled—in the interest of the king's safety.

The only one left was Moussoci, the mulatto engineer. He stood by the tyrant on the parapet of the Citadel and praised his work. "No one could discover the mechanism unless he were shown it. I have made it perfect."

"How many people know the secret?" asked the king.

"Only we two," answered Moussoci proudly.

"Good," said Christophe, and his companion screamed. There was no sound as the mangled body struck the rocks below.

"Now the secret is mine alone," the king murmured happily.

Proudly the finished edifice towered towards the sky. The hungry mouths of the cannon stuck out from the loopholes pointing in every direction of the compass. The munition rooms were full to bursting; La Ferrière was impregnable.

One day a terrible storm swept over the fortress. Blinding flashes of lightning zigzagged through the clouds; great bursts of thunder shook the building to its foundations. Christophe's savage nature yelled defiance at the roaring elements.

"Aha!" he shouted. "The Almighty thinks that *He* can intimidate King Christophe. *Mille tonnerres! I* will show Him how to make La Ferrière tremble. Turn out! To the cannons! Load every gun!

"Fire!

"Reload!

"Fire!

"Finish the ammunition to the last round! Let the Almighty get as good as He gives. *I*, the King, will show you how to shatter the foundations of the earth!"

Again and again the great cannons thundered their salute across the wilderness, drowning the fury of the storm. Through the endless galleries the gunners toiled like black demons in the sulphurous smoke.

Unbounded happiness filled the king's heart. He had matched the elements and silenced the voice of Heaven.

Throughout the kingdom his black majesty was surrounded with pomp and luxury. He built twenty palaces; each new one more magnificent than the last. The finest of them was Sans Souci, which he copied partly from the palace of Frederick the Great whom he admired more than any other ruler in the history of the world.

The best artists and scholars from Europe were welcomed at the royal court with open arms and rich hospitality. Sir Home Riggs Popham, the English admiral, visited Christophe at Sans Souci. The correct, precise bearing of the admiral made a profound impression upon the effervescent nature of the despot who gave Popham his whole-hearted friendship.

In the summer of 1820 the two of them were sitting on the balcony of the palace, enjoying the wonderful landscape spread before them and chatting quietly.

"Tell me, Henri," said the Englishman, "people say that you've become a hard-hearted tyrant. Is that true?"

There was silence. Christophe's great fist opened and clenched slowly. He made a gesture of helplessness. Of late his features had become sunken and furrowed; great troubles weighed upon him. Then he sighed and spoke.

"What else could I have done? Iron severity even to the point of cruelty was needed to lift my people up and give them a new life. I know that only fear can hold the human beast in check. Haiti needed and still needs a strong arm.

"It has not been easy. I am surrounded by traitors. Only a few days ago I discovered that Brelle, my French chaplain, had betrayed me to his country. Overwhelming proof was found hidden in his vestments—letters from France. Today he will be executed. Is *that* tyranny, Sir Home?"

In the lowlands the ferment began. At Cap Haitien they shouted "*À bas le Roi.*" They had never forgiven Christophe for his work during the revolution against the French, when he burned to the ground the most beautiful town in the Antilles.

There were whispers of revolt and the king's own kinsman, Duc de Marmalade, was the leader of the traitors. He had grossly misused his responsibility, and now, fearing retribution, he incited the natives secretly against their sovereign, urging them to break into open rebellion.

One incident will suffice to show how serious the trouble was. An Austrian ship sailed into the barbor of Cap Haitien and the duke compelled its owner, Baron von Dietrich, to surrender all his guns and ammunition in exchange for a cargo of coffee. The weapons were distributed among the malcontents.

Spies reported the news to Christophe and he, in a blind rage, ordered the death of the Austrian.

Marmalade tore up the warrant with a laugh.

The tyrant was no longer feared, and *that* was the beginning of the end.

In the tumble-down village church of St. Anne in Limonade, a few hours' ride from Sans Souci, Mass was being said before a small congregation. Suddenly came the clatter of hoofs and a horseman pulled up before the porch. He dismounted, strode in through the open door and walked with heavy tread up to the altar steps. There he knelt down and buried his face in his hands.

"*Le roi!*"—the whisper ran through the congregation. The priest stopped reading and the people stared in frightened silence at the bowed figure. What had driven the king to take sanctuary in this little church?

Dark thoughts tormented him. He knew that the end was near, and now the shadows of the past were haunting him. There was his Father Confessor whom he had had executed. And Gaffie, the executioner, who had held out the bleeding head to him under the great mango tree at Sans Souci. Should he repent that he in his passion had killed a servant of God? How should *he* know what was right? His brain was a mist of scarlet. Blood—blood—his whole life had led through rivers of blood. Revolution . . . La Ferrière . . . executions . . . whippings . . . God! Was there no end?

The priest, who had no idea of the terrible thoughts that ran through that tortured brain but imagined that the king had come to receive Communion, lifted the chalice from the altar and held it on high. Christophe raised his head, his eyes stared wide, his hand pointed with horror at the purple wine.

Yellow foam oozed out between his fleshy lips—there came a madman's scream: "*Brelle!!*" Slowly the enormous body straightened up. The great hands gripped the *prie-dieu* till it cracked. Now he stood erect, a black giant whose ill-fitting uniform hung loosely from his frame. His lips moved silently.

He swayed and pitched forward on the floor. Blood trickled from the back of his head where it had struck the edge of a desk. Still no one moved. . . .

Two hours later Dr. Duncan Stewart, the white doctor at Sans Souci, announced that the king lay unconscious from an apoplectic fit.

On the third morning Christophe opened his eyes.

He had lost the two most decisive days of his life. There was no time to be wasted. He tried to sit up in bed. His muscles refused to work; he was a cripple! Hurriedly a Papaloi was sent for. The English doctor said there was no cure, but a negro could work wonders with his herbs and fetishes. The king was lifted into hot baths of tobacco plants and rum. A little strength returned. He could just move his legs. There was still hope.

Muffled drum-beats throbbed through the air, spreading the news abroad that the tyrant was paralyzed. Christophe was helpless and his enemies rejoiced. Down in the lowlands the drunken crowds cheered and shouted, "A holiday—a holiday! No more work!"

The curtain of fear was lifting. The tight clenched fingers of the iron hand had started to relax.

St. Marc rebelled openly and again the drums pounded, sending their rousing message throughout the land, even to the most distant villages.

Christophe heard the drums and he too knew what they meant. He sent a regiment of soldiers under the command of his most trustworthy general, Jean Claude, to suppress the riot. On the way to St. Marc the soldiers turned on their commanding officer and murdered him. His head wrapped in a white cloth was sent back to the king. It was a signal of open defiance, but far from crushing Christophe it roused him to a last and desperate effort. No underling was to be trusted. The king must wield his own authority.

Laboriously he propped himself up in bed and called his secretary.

"Vastey," he said, "there is no time to be lost. Announce my royal intention that I myself will take the parade of the army tomorrow."

The people must yet be made to fear him; to fear him as a living corpse who could still use his voice, still move his fingers, and still keep his head.

He must succeed. The Papaloi was again summoned to use his utmost artifices in order that the king might be strong enough for his effort on the morrow. More hot baths, more fetishes, more incantations. . . . And the great man gathered every ounce of will-power he possessed to steel himself for the great ordeal. Everything depended upon it; by that one moment, and none knew better than Christophe himself, his kingdom stood or fell.

The hour for the inspection had arrived. Vast crowds stood round the parade ground, for the astonishing news had traveled fast and far. A deep hum of chatter, half nervous, half defiant, arose from the assembled mob. Suddenly the trumpets blared out, the palace gates opened and a deadly silence fell. The regiments stood ready, rank upon rank in deep unwavering lines.

Then from out of the great doorway stepped the king, resplendent in his white uniform, gold epaulettes, and crimson sash. A gasp went up. They had never expected this. The man still lived; they had witnessed a miracle.

"*Vive le Roi. Vive l'homme Christophe. Vive . . .*" yelled the crowds, frantic in their excitement.

A voice of thunder quelled the uproar.

"My horse!"

The royal white Arab was led forward. The critical moment had arrived and more than a negro kingdom hung in the balance. A last supreme effort must be made. The veins on Christophe's forehead swelled to thick pulsing cords, the only evidence of the terrible struggle that was being fought between an iron will and a paralyzed body.

With two . . . three . . . four long swaying strides the king stood beside his horse. A sigh ran round the multitude, a sigh of awe and re-awakening fear. Their emperor had risen from the dead. His hand grasped at the pommel of the saddle and with a sudden effort he reached for the stirrup iron. Poised for an eternity and then—the mighty form crumpled like an empty sack upon the ground.

The game was up.

Tears rolled down Christophe's cheeks as he sat again in his room, defeated. On either side stood Dr. Stewart and his Haitian assistant Dr. Denneau. They had been true friends for many years and he could pour out his heart to them.

"The old firebrand Toussaint and I . . . we once dreamed of doing great deeds, and oh! . . . we have . . . done . . . so little."

Then, after a pause: "Do you know, my friends—it's cold and lonely up there. . . . The storm blows and the wind howls, and the higher a man climbs up the lofty mountains of immortality the lonelier he feels. Even I have found it lonely. The highest summit is reached only by a few, so very few . . ."

Deep in thought, thoughts that were now so bitter, he continued murmuring to himself: "And still so much to do . . ."

Outside the windows the skies reddened in the reflection of the fires. The army had long since disbanded and joined the murdering pillaging mob.

"*À bas le Roi!*"—the shout rang through Haiti, echoed by a hundred thousand voices.

"*Egalité! Vive l'independence!*" bawled the drunken crowd.

Bullets whistled through the air and the revolution rolled on like an avalanche along the royal highway, towards Sans Souci, towards the king.

It was time to go. Christophe bade farewell to his family and dearest friends and sent them forth in safety. He was staying, to greet for the last time his ungrateful subjects.

Beside the chair in which the king sat was an ebony cabinet, beautifully inlaid with mother-of-pearl. Christophe pulled open the top drawer and took out a little gold-chased pistol and a golden bullet. Carefully he pushed the bullet into the barrel and primed the pistol. . . .

The first plundering hordes were already in the palace. Shouting and yelling they destroyed everything that lay in their way.

A shot rang out from the king's room.

Christophe lay on the floor and a vivid trail of scarlet crept down his white silk nightshirt.

A window flew open over the courtyard and a voice—shrill with terror and rage—rang out.

"*Le Roi est mort.*"

The words ran from mouth to mouth. There was a lull and then the shouting grew to a deafening roar: "*Liberté! Independence! . . .*"

"*Le Roi d'Haiti est mort.*"

The king's last adherents fled along the secret passage to La Ferrière bearing Christophe's heavy, lifeless body.

The Citadel was empty. Even the garrison, the most faithful men in the army, had deserted and gone down to the valley below. The unearthly silence of the fortress drove the fugitives to the near edge of madness as they searched desperately for a last safe resting place wherein to lay the king. At last they discovered an open chalk grave in the middle of the courtyard and into this they lowered the body. It was not quite deep enough. A black, clenched fist still stuck out of the white hole, threatening the sky. As well as they could the men filled in the grave and built a little sarcophagus-like hut over the dead hand.

It was the same hut against which I now leant, drinking my coffee and thinking of the past.

There came into my mind the words of "L'Immortalité," a song written by the Comte des Rosier for Christophe's "Temple de Memoire":

Héros, Chéri de la victoire
Léve, Henri! Ton front radieux?
Digne favori de la gloire!
Tu comptes au nombre des Dieux.
Ouvre tes exploits glorieux
Et les neufs soeurs de ton histoire
Vont remplir la voûte des cieux.
Gloire à Henri! Chantons ce sublime génie;
Honneurs a ses divins Lauriers!
Et que la céleste harmonie
Repete: Vive Henri le plus Grand des Guerriers!

The iron fists of La Ferrière still tower into the clouds today, a symbol of what has been. . . .

The wind howled and whistled through the galleries. Bats swooped like dead souls over the castle and courtyard. Black, threatening clouds wrapped round the mountain. And there, behind me, beat the stone heart of the greatest negro that ever lived. Forgotten by his people, but not by the world.

I shivered for it was getting cold. My hand reached for the rum bottle and as I tipped it to my mouth the soothing spirit ran through my veins like fire. I propped up my wrist-watch on a niche in the King's tomb so that I could see the luminous dial plainly. Then I pushed the revolver under the one blanket rolled up as a pillow; the other I wrapped round me. Now I was ready for sleep.

The fire sank gradually lower and in a little while a sudden puff of wind swept the last sparks far into the air above the Citadel.

It was dark.

X. BLACK MAGIC

WHEREVER I went in Haiti, and my stay there lasted several months, I was dumfounded at the universal spread of Voodoo. At almost every step I was reminded of the actual and practical existence of this primitive African religion.

In Port-au-Prince, in Jérémie, in the depths of the jungle, everywhere stood the dread symbol of Voodoo. The first time I saw it was by the Massacre River. A solitary hut stood in a little clearing on the bank and in front of the hut was a pole stuck in the ground with a bleached horse skull on the top. This grisly ornament serves, according to Haitian belief, to ward off the "Duppies," evil spirits of the dead.

These Duppies are extremely dangerous. They lurk chiefly in the neighborhood of graves and have to be continually

In front of the hut was a pole with a bleached horse skull on the top

TRIFIXION

6 6

6

DEICIDE

appeased by offerings of food and drink. When I was in the Plaine de Gonaïves I examined many of the curious tombstones there. Everyone was built with sacrificial niches round it, and it was rarely that I found a niche which did not contain some remnants of dried food and a bottle of wine.

But Voodoo is not only passive propitiation; it is a fiendishly active cult. In every town one or more houses are to be seen whose walls are covered with symbolic figures painted in crude, glaring colors. These are the congregating places for the worshipers. What happens inside none but the initiates know.

Over the whole land is stretched a net of secret terror in whose meshes the Haitian negro is helplessly entangled; and the priests of Voodoo, the Papaloi and Mamaloi, having all the drawlines in their hands, keep the natives in a state of deep subservience and fear. Thus they retain their evil and absolute power over the masses.

Whenever I tried to bring the conversation round to the subject of Voodoo, I always met with the same result: the common native fell into a state of dumb terror, almost a trance; the educated negro became embarrassed. Either way, the answer was silence.

I remember especially clearly a talk which I had with "Uncle Dave," a negro whom I met in Port-au-Prince. "Uncle Dave" had once been a brigadier-general in the Haitian army, but he had come down in the world and he now earned a meager pittance as machine cleaner in the cotton factory of one of my acquaintances. This friendly old man, with his strange wrinkled face, was an ardent Voodooist, so I hoped that I might discover something from him about this cult which is as old as the negro race itself.

I sat down beside him in the shadow of his hut on the

Rue de Quai. He began talking at first about his childhood; of Jamaica where he had been born; how he had come to Haiti, and how, in the shadow of Voodoo, he climbed to success like a liana round a palm tree. At the mention of Voodoo I tried to draw him out on the subject. I did not expect details for I knew too much about the negro temperament, but I at least hoped for some vague indications as to the basic beliefs of his religion. He proved quite willing to treat me to a little monologue.

"Monsieur," he began, "if you live long enough on this island even you won't be able to escape the spirits which inhabit it. They will pursue you until they catch your soul and possess your body. You're powerless against them; only the Papaloi and the holy priestesses, the Mamaloi, can control them and protect you from disaster.

"Worship the Green Snake for she is holy, and in her dwells the soul of Damballa. Damballa the almighty on whose right hand sits Ezilée, his mistress. They are the great gods. Only they can defend you from the terrible blood-smeared demon, Ogoun Badagris.

"Listen to the beat of the Voodoo drums and worship with the Faithful. Follow the gentle call and Papa Legba, the all-gracious, will shelter you in his mercy. But sometimes the air throbs with the muffled poundings of the great Rada drums, and then you know that Ogoun Badagris must be appeased. Then you must go forth into the kingdom of Loco, god of the jungle, and at midnight you will receive with your brother sinners the baptism of blood. Only the blood sacrifice can cleanse your sinful bodies and prepare them for the dwelling place of the all-wise Damballa.

"Voodoo is strong; stronger even than death.

"The Papaloi can raise the dead. He breathes life into

corpses, who get up and behave like living men. These creatures are bound forever to their master's will. They are called 'Zombies.' Don't look at me so incredulously, monsieur. Of course there are Zombies. Haven't you noticed how even the poorest natives bury their dead under a heavy stone? That's a very necessary precaution, for it stops the bodies from leaving their graves. And then tell me—why do the relatives of the dead man or woman sit night and day for a whole week upon the tomb? Why!—just to make sure the body decays!

"Don't you realize, monsieur, that many of the workers on the sugar fields are mere soulless carcasses, brought back to life by magic and now slaving for their masters? Several times I have seen the black spirits flying away overhead. I swear it; I saw them with my own eyes. No one can escape from the terrible powers of evil. You may laugh and sneer, but every word I tell you is true.

"Yes, monsieur—you must first live many years in Haiti and then things will be plain to you at which you now scoff. There are terrible things and beautiful things of which you have no conception. But one thing even you know: Voodoo is a devilish cult . . . dangerous and devilish. . . ."

"Magic?"

Herr Direktor Henckel leaned pensively back in his bamboo chair and crossed his hands behind his head.

"I don't know. . . . Do you call it magic when we receive invisible and inaudible vibrations of the ether with our delicate instruments and turn them into music? Is it magic when we hear the same voice at the same time in London, Berlin, New York, and Tokyo? The learned have their formulæ for these technical wonders; the common herd accept them, without thinking or criticizing, as a *fait accompli* beyond their powers of comprehension.

"So in Voodoo, there are mysteries which need explanation. There are certain secrets which are more easily accepted by a primitive, earth-bound people than by an over-civilized nation. . . ."

We were sitting on the veranda of the Mariani Country Club, on the slopes above Port-au-Prince. From the smoking room came the tinkle of ice as the negro bartenders busied themselves mixing "swizzles." Sounds of naked footsteps and feminine laughter carried across the intervening darkness. The veranda was quiet when Henckel stopped speaking. By day one got a magnificent view from here, but now there was only the dim bulk of Port-au-Prince in the darkness below, pricked out with the tiny yellow points of its scattered lights; and behind us loomed the jagged silhouette of the distant mountains. It was a time and place conducive to talk, perched as we were halfway between the hills and the sea, surrounded by illimitable night, and comforted in the knowledge of human companionship by the chatter from the barroom at the back.

It was no mere chance that I was sitting beside Henckel on this evening, for whenever, during my stay in Haiti, I had broached the subject of Voodoo, I had always received the same advice: "When you get back to Port-au-Prince, ask Henckel. *He* knows."

Henckel was a German. He had been born at Frankfurt, but at an early age he had emigrated to Haiti and entered the dyewoods business. Consequently, in the course of his duties, he had spent many years in the jungle and through continual association and living with the negroes it naturally happened that he heard a lot about Voodoo. From the first he had taken a keen interest in the cult, studying it closely, and he had probably delved deeper into the negro mentality than any other white man before him.

I heard all this before I ever saw him and it made me all the more eager to meet him. Therefore, as soon as I returned to Port-au-Prince from La Ferrière, I engineered an introduction to this remarkable man, and since we had much in common, including our nationality and language, I spent many enthralling hours in his company.

It was the first evening. We had just dined together and now we were sitting outside in the warm darkness, puffing at our cigars. A white-coated waiter brought us a carafe of "Rhum Barbancourt" and two glasses. Henckel filled them up and handed one to me. Then he lay back, sipping his drink in silence. I was longing to ask him some questions, but I thought it would be wiser to wait until he was ready to speak. A few more minutes' silence; suddenly he sat up and placed his glass on the bamboo table beside him. He ran his stumpy fingers through his sparse white hair and turned towards me.

"How long have you been here? Only a few months! And I—well—it's forty years since I came over from Costa Rica. When one has lived here as long as I have, one becomes wonderfully intimate with the land and its people. . . .

"Of course, black Haiti without Voodoo is inconceivable. Voodoo regulates the life, politics, outlook, and social and family relationships of the Haitian. It is, in actual fact, the real religion of the country, although Roman Catholicism is recognized as such. But Catholicism never stood a chance against Voodoo. In the native mind the Cross plays a pitiful rôle beside the fetishes and the Green Snake. The priest has always been foreign to Haitian ways; he has never tried to understand or make allowance for them, and consequently, in any case of difficulty, disease, or danger, it is always the Papaloi who is summoned, and no one else.

"The beliefs of Voodoo have been created expressly for the African soul and they are therefore understandable to the negro, unlike the Christian teachings of the white men. The negro is much closer to the earth than we whites, and his nature is more easily swayed by elemental influences.

"You said you explored the jungle along the Massacre River. Didn't the vastness of tropical nature amaze and overwhelm you? You, as an artist, have a discerning eye and a keen ear for the creation and evolution of nature. You translate *your* impressions into lines and colors, the negro translates *his* into a hierarchy of gods as old as his race. The white man looks down to nature, the negro looks up at it. That is the great and basic difference between the black and white mentality.

"Voodoo is the perfect expression of the native soul. It was the only cult which the enslaved negroes brought from Africa to Haiti, and it proved to them a constant source of comfort and hope, even through their darkest days. And when the time for rebellion came, it needed a strong foundation of religion to raise the oppressed slaves from their apathy and to unite them in the fight for freedom. The first drumbeats of revolt throbbed out at a Voodoo celebration in the forest near Bois Caiman and, in the name of Voodoo, a massacre of the white men followed.

"The first ruler under the new régime of freedom soon realized that the Voodoo priests were the real masters of the island. No wonder Toussaint l'Ouverture tried to assure his power by suppressing theirs. His efforts to stamp out this bestial religion were in vain. Even his nearest followers came under its sway and some of them actually took the office of Papaloi. The domination of Voodoo in Haiti lasted for a hundred years, during which period the white man was almost completely excluded from the island and little or no news trickled through to the outer world.

"Even under the governorship of Geffrard, the mulatto president, the priests retained their ascendency in spite of the efforts made by this progressive ruler to exterminate them. There was one episode when Geffrard caught the participators in a disgusting cannibal orgy. They were condemned to be executed. Scarcely had the echoes of the volley died away, when a well-aimed bullet flew through a church window and killed the President's only daughter. It was no use resisting. . . .

"Today the power of Voodoo is as great as it ever was. One might say with certainty that ninety-five per cent of the black population are in varying degrees adherents, active or passive, of the cult. Christianity knows no magic words such as the superstitious negro wants. It has no evil fetishes which are the essence of every native religion. The Catholic priest inspires no fear. But the Papaloi can take a man's life and soul and bewitch or destroy his family. The Papaloi is, at the same time, patriarch and doctor; he heals the sick and comforts the love-lorn. If a man wants vengeance on his enemy he goes to the Papaloi. At birth, marriage, and death—the Papaloi is always summoned.

"One can think what one likes about the efficacy of Voodoo ritual, but it cannot be denied that it has a powerful sensual appeal and that, as far as the negro is concerned, is all he wants. He understands and puts his trust in it.

"The true Haitian is a Romanic African, but in him the Romanic civilization is scarcely more than skin deep and from under this thin veneer the ancient African nature forces its way out like a volcano from beneath the crust of the earth. We Haitians feel within us the deep, secret forces that control our lives. I say *we* intentionally, for in me too the subconscious primitive nature has been unloosed through constant association with natives. In the still, velvet night when the ever-changing rhythm of the holy dance enwraps our souls with its magic thrall, strange spiritual eruptions are unpent, releasing suppressed and sleeping passions and metaphysical powers.

"This is an island whose inhabitants are free from all the sham morality of modern civilization. The young negro when he woos a girl, approaches her with the phallic bull's horns on his forehead; a typical example of the innocent naked eroticism of the African native.

"Take for instance 'Ouanga.' Perhaps you don't know what that is? It's simply a love fetish. Supposing the love of a young man is not reciprocated by the object of his affection; he will go to the Papaloi for help. The magician takes two sewing-needles, lays them side by side, point to eye, and binds them tightly together with strands of wool, round which is wrapped a layer of medicine-leaves. The finished amulet is sewn in a leather pouch and worn round the neck. In the case of a girl, she goes to the Mamaloi, but the ceremony is the same. All Haiti swears by 'Ouanga.'

"The priestly caste has inherited from generation to generation a profound knowledge of healing, and it would be stupid to doubt the efficacy of many of their cures. I know diseases which any white doctor would pronounce incurable, and yet a Voodoo priest would take their cure for granted. I

The young negro when he woos a girl; a typical example of the innocent, naked eroticism of the African native

myself would never summon a European doctor except for a case which necessitated surgical operation. For everything else I trust to nature and it must be admitted that the Papaloi have an unparalleled knowledge of natural healing.

"If a priest is faced with some illness beyond the capacity of his nature-medicines, he drags in all sorts of hocus-pocus, incantations, fetishes, and so forth—*not* because he really believes that they have magic powers, but because he understands the mental equipment of his patient. He is a first-rate psychologist and he realizes that he needs these rigmaroles to soothe the sick man, just as a European doctor needs *his* hocus-pocus, albeit in a slightly different form. . . .

"The mysterious machinations of the Voodoo priests extend into yet another realm, that of the transcendental. The Papaloi have, like the Indian Yogis, an amazing knowledge of hypnosis and suggestion. In fact, their powers are so great that they can bring death upon the man who defies or thwarts them. I myself have repeatedly witnessed such cases. Once I saw an apparently healthy man fall to the ground and writhe out his death agonies, while at the same time and several miles away a Papaloi squatted in silent concentration on the floor of a Houmfort, cursing the man's life away.

"Such phenomena cannot be explained by simply shrugging the shoulders. The white man may laugh at such things and turn away, but a negro whose soul is filled with secret terrors knows otherwise. Still, whatever you think, it is best for a stranger in Haiti to have as many friends and as few enemies as possible.

"From the first day of my life in Haiti I tried to approach and understand the simple mind of the negro. I was young then and I lived for years on end in the jungle at a time when no other white man dared leave the coast. The natives understood me and treated me as one of themselves. I listened to their murmured conversations and I watched them closely, especially when they brought the drums out of their grass huts and danced and sang to an age-old melody that at some distant time and place had poured from a primitive soul. Under such conditions what could a lonely white man do but lead the life of a native? I became the chosen favorite of a Mamaloi, a beautiful young negress whose passionate love was only exceeded by her religious fanaticism. Thus I came to take part in all the ritual ceremonies. The Voodoo fire held me in thrall. With a red wig on my head I danced as madly as the blacks themselves. I became heart and soul a Voodooist. . . .

"And yet—there was a last boundary that I could not cross. I don't need to assure you that I never took part in, never saw, and never wittingly countenanced a human sacrifice.

"One day I heard that a great ceremonial feast was imminent to which all the negroes from far and near were hastening. A certain uneasiness amongst the natives made me suspicious. Something unusual was in the wind. How the idea first occurred to me I don't know, but I couldn't get rid of the awful fear that a ritual murder was going to take place. Not that I had any anxiety lest *I* might have been chosen as a victim. It was the thought of being a witness to this crime that filled me with such unutterable disgust. There was only one thing to do. I went to the Mamaloi and questioned her openly on the subject. I told her that I would do everything in my power to prevent a sacrifice if such had been planned.

"She listened in silence. Then she smiled and answered: 'It is ridiculous what you say. You are feverish. Come into my hut and I'll make you a soothing drink.' She was so calm in the face of my accusation that I realized I must have been wrong. So I sat in the doorway of her hut and listened to her gay chatter and sipped the delicious brew of herbs she had prepared for me.

"Thirty-six hours later I awoke. I was alone in the hut. Outside, the natives were in an extraordinary state of excitement and hysteria. No amount of questioning could elicit the story of what happened on the previous night. I was furious with the Mamaloi for having deceived me and given me a sleeping draught and I broke off my friendship with her completely. It was a relief when, a few days later, the order came for me to return to the coast and supervise the building of a new warehouse.

"Inquiries which I made later confirmed my suspicions that several human sacrifices had taken place on that fateful night.

"I believe that there is a certain sect of fanatics who regard the dismembering and eating of children as part of the Voodoo ritual, but although these pathological exceptions do exist I am certain that the great majority of the worshipers detest and abhor such bestial orgies.

"Animal sacrifices come into a different category altogether, for they are still in universal practice. Throughout the land hens and goats are slaughtered at all the more important feasts. The blood cult is the oldest of all cults and penetrates all boundaries of race and age. The symbolism of blood is recognized and incorporated even in our civilized Christianity. But with us it remains symbolic. To the negro a sacrifice has a double aspect. It has a ritual meaning (as in every religion) *and* a physical meaning. Therefore, when considering the effect of animal sacrifice, it is essential to remember the terrific stimulus which the sensuous African mind receives at the sight of running blood.

"Voodoo is supreme. The Christian missionaries of a dozen different denominations may go on fighting to suppress the ancient dances and rituals. They will never succeed. Haiti is, and always will be—Haiti!"

Henckel's pipe had long since gone out but he still held it clasped between his hands. We gazed in silence over the sleeping town, now almost in darkness.

From the mountains behind came the muffled beat of a drum.

XI. VOODOO FIRE

As WE rode through the night the drums were beating again—but with a new rhythm that I had never heard before. I was keyed up to a pitch of perspiring excitement, fearing what was to come and yet unwilling to turn back. We were about to participate in a monstrous performance, an orgy which not one white man in a million has ever seen. Tonight was a Voodoo Fire, and *we* were to be present.

That same morning I had arrived in Jacmel, where Henckel's coffee plantation lay. The German had, during the course of our conversations in Port-au-Prince, invited me to come and stay with him. He had mentioned at the time that I might be able to learn a few interesting facts about Voodoo, but as I traveled south, I never imagined for a moment that it would be possible to visit one of those negro festivals. At the most, I hoped to be introduced to someone, perhaps a Papaloi, who could give me an eye-witness account of the ritual procedure. But it never entered my head that I, a white man unknown to the natives, would be allowed to see . . . to see what?

I shivered as I rode along. I was horribly afraid; afraid of the night, afraid of the menacing drums, and above all, afraid of seeing *too much.*

On the afternoon of my arrival the overseer had come to Henckel with a message and they had talked together in the study for over an hour. When the man had gone, my host told me that a great ceremonial dance was to be held that evening in a forest clearing about fifteen miles from the plantation. Would I care to come? It was too great an opportunity to be missed, so in spite of inward misgivings I agreed.

We set out at sunset and now we were trotting through the darkness towards the mountains. The air was hot and heavy and trembled with the distant echo of the drums. We entered Jacmel and passed through the market place. The only illumination in the square were tiny oil lamps which threw a murky, ineffective glimmer over the dingy wares displayed on upturned boxes and petrol tins. Behind each stall squatted a white-clad figure. The chatter turned to an ominous silence as we rode by and they all stared at us with sullen curiosity. I hoped that our reception at the feast would be more friendly. . . .

The path climbed upward amongst the jagged hills. Below us lay the town and, far off, the sea, glittering in the moonlight. It was a warm night, yet the pale rays of the moon cast a chill aura of malignant evil over the scene. We rode through a cemetery where the whitewashed tombstones flitted past like serried ranks of ghosts, then the dark shape of trees rose up again on either side, stretching their gnarled branches in our way.

And all the while the hollow booming of the drums rang in our ears; now nearer, now further off, rising and falling in subtle cadences. Often it seemed as if the sound were no more than half a mile away and then it faded into a distant throb. Strange . . . the nearer we approached, the fainter it became. But it never died completely away nor ever varied its rhythm. There were two distinct phases in the refrain. First the short, staccato: *Tom-ti-ti-tom* . . . luring and enticing; then the surging, heavy *Booom-boom,* threatening and compelling. The drums were calling, they drugged the will until all resistance died. I realized with impotent horror that it was impossible to turn back; the power of the drums was too great.

But which way now? Henckel seemed to know. We turned off into a narrow bush path where the branches laced overhead into a vast natural corridor. Myriads of glow-worms flitted through the trees. Strange creatures scuttled off as we forced the undergrowth aside. Forwards—there was no escape. We pressed on, hurrying faster and faster to reach the end.

Suddenly we emerged into a wide clearing. In the middle was a huge fire and round about it were assembled at least two hundred negroes and negresses. Our arrival was scarcely noticed. Everyone seemed to know Henckel, and as for me—I was his friend.

For the most part the blacks were squatting on the ground, chanting songs of immemorial antiquity whilst their bodies swayed from side to side to the throb of the music. A man strode to the center of the circle and stirred up the fire into a roaring blaze.

It was a picture of primeval Africa: the solemn incantations, the swaying black bodies bronzed in the liquid glow of the flames, and the numbing beat of the drums. The intoxication of sound and sight had invaded my senses. The scorching heat of the flames filled me with an overpowering lassitude. I squatted down beside Henckel and waited.

To the left of the fire a row of stakes had been driven into the ground. Fixed horizontally across them at the height of a man's head were crossbars from which depended five long conical drums. A gigantic naked negro stood in front of each, working like a fiend. Two of the men used short wooden sticks but the other three evoked a peculiar rhythm by gliding their fingers and palms over the tightly stretched goatskins. The drums responded to the efforts of these sweating blacks with a shattering resonance of sound.

A sinewy youth whose tall slim form was clad only in a pair of loose white cotton trousers bounded into the center of the circle and stood for a moment outlined against the leaping background of flames. Suddenly he sprung into the air, pirouetting like a madman and, as his feet touched the ground again, stopped dead, poised motionless as a statue. Then, conscious to very finger tips of the rôle he was playing, he strutted solemnly up and down in the arena, a rampant cock of the roost. All at once his movements became supple and alluring; perfectly feminine, like a woman in rapturous surrender. He minced to and fro a few times and then again his body jerked erect, tense and thrusting, fiercely responding to the crescendo of the drums.

It was a demonstration of pure sexuality; an unadorned

exhibition of that masculinity which the white man, in contrast to the negro, so carefully conceals.

The moon climbed up the sky, painting the tree tops with its silver light.

A last thud, and the drums were silent.

The crowd divided and a procession of negresses, bearing great bowls of steaming food, walked into the center and up to the fire and laid their bowls at equal intervals round the circumference of the blaze. Then they retired, all except one who, accompanied by the syncopated tapping of a little drum, sang:

Damballa goubamba
Kinga do ki la.

The crowd chanted the response: *Kinga do ki la*, clapping their hands at every syllable.

Suddenly a negress wearing a white chemise and a scarlet sash stood up. It was the Mamaloi. She began to dance. Now the big drums had taken up the beat, thudding in an unchanging monotone. Never higher, never lower, always the same . . . vibrating and pulsing through the darkness . . . there was no resisting their insidious power. The sound drove mercilessly through the still air, coursing through the veins like a hot fever, sapping all energy and self-control. . . .

Backwards and forwards danced the Mamaloi. In and out between the rows of squatting figures. Her eyes were fixed in a rigid sightless stare and the sweat poured down her body. Saliva ran from her mouth, trickling down her neck and between her breasts. She approached the fire. On the ground stood the basins of food, congo beans, ground rice, watermelons, and jugs of tafia, the fiery Haitian rum. From a shallow dish the priestess sprinkled water over the repast.

The singing became louder—the bass drums pounded faster—*Boom—boom—boom*, threaded always with the sharp tormenting staccato beats.

My God! Would this *never* stop? . . .

Like a lustful tigress the Mamaloi wound her way between the rows of chanting men and women. She was approaching me. She stood in front of me, naked. Unwillingly I rose to my feet. Her eyes held mine as she swayed there. Her quivering body almost touched me. I felt a fierce impulse to spring forward. . . . Then she was gone. She stood now at the further side, her arms outstretched over the ranks of woolly heads, as if she would raise each sensuous body into her own state of orgiastic frenzy.

This mass suggestion had the desired effect. The eyes that followed her in her maze of twistings and turnings became rigid in their gaze; the heavy air made breathing difficult; a cloudy haze swept across the senses. In front of the fire the mad contortions of the dancer came to a sudden end. She stood for a moment, head thrown back, mouth open, her beautiful pear-shaped breasts proudly thrust forward—a perfect statue in bronze. The roaring flames behind seemed to draw out elemental and uncontrollable emotions which writhed upwards through her body, escaping from her mouth.

A violent fit of trembling shook the woman. It was as if a demon lover had taken possession of her and were exploring her limbs to their very extremities. Someone handed her a black cock which she raised high above her head. The scene was diabolical. There stood the naked negress, her sweat-streaked body glistening in the ruddy firelight, and at arm's length she held a terrified black cock, the very symbol of Satan, squawking and flapping its wings, while the feathers flew in all directions. An awful sickness gripped me. I felt as if I were looking into the very depths of evil. The thunder of the drums grew to an avalanche of deafening reverberations.

Slowly the body of the Mamaloi relaxed from its rigid posture. She began to turn; faster—faster—faster. Like a madman she spun round on her toes. She swung the cock now only by its legs and as it flew through the air in dizzy circles it spread its wings wide in the last convulsions of death. As though carried through the air by the beating pinions the negress whirled forwards in frantic ecstasy. The drums rose to their shattering finale, the woman stopped motionless, and then—a miracle—the dying cock twisted its neck convulsively and crowed—crowed loud and raucous into the surrounding night. It was the final touch of horror.

A sigh of relief surged over the crowd. I tried to look away for I suddenly knew what was about to happen. It was no use; my gaze was fixed as in a hypnotic trance upon the negress and her sacrifice.

Unexpectedly the bright blade of a machete flashed through the air. The cock's head flew in a wide circle to the earth. Quick as thought, before a drop of the precious liquid should be spilt, the Mamaloi pushed the bleeding neck into her mouth and sucked the blood out of the twitching body. Her teeth were dyed crimson. Blood ran over her chin, her throat, her breasts, and down her thighs.

Shrill screams of hysteria burst from the onlookers.

New cocks were brought forward and slaughtered. The Papalois caught the spouting blood in bowls and sprinkled it over the frenzied crowd who struggled and fought to be anointed. It was the great purification. Only after a baptism of blood can the good spirit Damballa enter the soul.

A broad-shouldered, athletic negro jumped up in front of me and shouted: "*Commençons! Dance Calinda! Boudum! Boudum!*"

The Mamaloi poured some rum into a basin, lit the spirit and with one sweep scattered the flaming blue liquid amongst the crowd on the ground. They yelled their delight and she did it again and again as she sang the wild Canga:

Eh! Eh! Bomba! Hen! Hen!
Canga bafio te
Canga moune de la
Canga do ki la
Canga li.

And the chorus bawled back:

Aia bombaia bombe!
Lama Samana quana!
Even, vante, a
Vans docki!

A solid ring of sweating, naked bodies formed round the fire. They were dancing the Calinda. More and more performers joined in, pressed close against one another, men and women, rubbing body to body in the red glow of the flames. The irregular circle of a hundred bodies molten into one Hydra-headed monster was carried along on jerking legs and stamping feet. The drums rolled faster, the black throng revolved with-ever increasing rapidity. Round and round they went as the ground shook under the impact of two hundred feet. . . .

The dance had passed its climax. It had achieved its object. Separate figures were breaking off from the main crowd and hurrying away into the darkness. I noticed that Henckel, who a moment before was sitting beside me, had vanished. My brain was too dazed to realize what had happened. Suddenly I found myself swept to my feet in the middle of a crowd of leaping, whirling couples; men and women, naked, screaming, white teeth grinning, lustfully moaning, irresistibly welded together in the erotic sensuality of the dance and the roaring fire.

One after another the drummers sank exhausted to the earth. But there was no lull. There were always fresh arms ready to take up the sticks and carry on the maddening refrain. . . .

The moon sank below the horizon. The open space was empty. Couples wrestled together in the darkness of the bush. . . . A few men stumbled by with arms full of brushwood which they piled upon the fire till the flames leaped up above the tops of the tall palms around us. There was no sound but the crackling of the dry sticks and the gasps of the straining figures as they celebrated the great rites of love.

The people vanished like ghosts. We were the last to go. . . . Hours later, as we turned round in our saddles, we could still see the crimson flames streaming against the black Haitian night. Henckel sat on his horse silent and lost in thought. A fierce struggle was going on inside him. What it was I dared not guess. We rode on again.

The cold gray light of dawn had just begun to dispel the darkness of night as we cantered into the empty streets of Jacmel. Henckel rode up beside me, laid one hand on my shoulder and with the other pointed to the distant flames. His eyes stared wearily into mine. His silent lips moved slowly:

"Voodoo Fire!"